POEMS

OF

THE ORIENT.

BY

BAYARD TAYLOR.

THIRD EDITION.

BOSTON:
TICKNOR AND FIELDS.
M DCCC LV.

STEREOTYPED AT THE
BOSTON STEREOTYPE FOUNDRY.

CONTENTS.

PROEM DEDICATORY.

POEMS OF THE ORIENT.

II.

PROEM DEDICATORY.

AN EPISTLE FROM MOUNT TMOLUS.

TO RICHARD HENRY STODDARD.

I.

O Friend, were you but couched on Tmolus' side,
In the warm myrtles, in the golden air
Of the declining day, which half lays bare,
Half drapes, the silent mountains and the wide
Embosomed vale, that wanders to the sea;
And the far sea, with doubtful specks of sail,
And farthest isles, that slumber tranquilly
Beneath the Ionian autumn's violet veil;—

Were you but with me, little were the need
  Of this imperfect artifice of rhyme,
  Where the strong Fancy peals a broken chime
And the ripe brain but sheds abortive seed.
But I am solitary, and the curse,
  Or blessing, which has clung to me from birth —
The torment and the ecstasy of verse —
  Comes up to me from the illustrious earth
Of ancient Tmolus; and the very stones,
Reverberant, din the mellow air with tones
Which the sweet air remembers; and they blend
  With fainter echoes, which the mountains fling
From far oracular caverns: so, my Friend,
          I cannot choose but sing!

II.

Unto mine eye, less plain the shepherds be,
  Tending their browsing goats amid the broom,
Or the slow camels, travelling towards the sea,
  Laden with bales from Baghdad's gaudy loom,
Or yon nomadic Turcomans, that go
  Down from their summer pastures — than the twain
Immortals, who on Tmolus' thymy top
  Sang, emulous, the rival strain!
Down the charmed air did light Apollo drop;

Great Pan ascended from the vales below.
I see them sitting in the silent glow ;
I hear the alternating measures flow
From pipe and golden lyre ; — the melody
  Heard by the Gods between their nectar bowls,
Or when, from out the chambers of the sea,
  Comes the triumphant Morning, and unrolls
A pathway for the sun ; then, following swift,
  The dædal harmonies of awful caves
Cleft in the hills, and forests that uplift
  Their sea-like boom, in answer to the waves,
With many a lighter strain, that dances o'er
The wedded reeds, till Echo strives in vain
          To follow :
        Hark ! once more,
      How floats the God's exultant strain
        In answer to Apollo !

"*The wind in the reeds and the rushes,*
  The bees on the bells of thyme,
The birds on the myrtle bushes,
  The cicàle above in the lime,
And the lizards below in the grass
Are as silent as ever old Tmolus was,
  Listening to my sweet pipings."

III.

I cannot separate the minstrels' worth;
  Each is alike transcendent and divine.
What were the Day, unless it lighted Earth?
  And what were Earth, should Day forget to shine?
But were you here, my Friend, we twain would build
  Two altars, on the mountain's sunward side:
  There Pan should o'er my sacrifice preside,
And there Apollo your oblation gild.
He is your God, but mine is shaggy Pan;
  Yet, as their music no discordance made,
  So shall our offerings side by side be laid,
And the same wind the rival incense fan.

IV.

You strain your ear to catch the harmonies
  That in some finer region have their birth;
I turn, despairing, from the quest of these,
  And seek to learn the native tongue of Earth.
In "Fancy's tropic clime" your castle stands,
  A shining miracle of rarest art;
I pitch my tent upon the naked sands,

And the tall palm, that plumes the orient lands,
  Can with its beauty satisfy my heart.
You, in your starry trances, breathe the air
  Of lost Elysium, pluck the snowy bells
  Of lotus and Olympian asphodels,
And bid us their diviner odors share.
I at the threshold of that world have lain,
  Gazed on its glory, heard the grand acclaim
  Wherewith its trumpets hail the sons of Fame,
And striven its speech to master — but in vain.
And now I turn, to find a late content
  In Nature, making mine her myriad shows;
  Better contented with one living rose
Than all the Gods' ambrosia; sternly bent
On wresting from her hand the cup, whence flow
  The flavors of her ruddiest life — the change
  Of climes and races — the unshackled range
Of all experience; — that my songs may show
The warm red blood that beats in hearts of men,
And those who read them in the festering den
  Of cities, may behold the open sky,
And hear the rhythm of the winds that blow,
  Instinct with Freedom. Blame me not, that I
Find in the forms of Earth a deeper joy
Than in the dreams which lured me as a boy,

And leave the Heavens, where you are wandering still
  With bright Apollo, to converse with Pan;
  For, though full soon our courses separate ran,
We, like the Gods, can meet on Tmolus' hill.

V.

There is no jealous rivalry in Song:
  I see your altar on the hill-top shine,
  And mine is built in shadows of the Pine,
Yet the same worships unto each belong.
Different the Gods, yet one the sacred awe
  Their presence brings us, one the reverent heart
Wherewith we honor the immortal law
  Of that high inspiration, which is Art.
Take, therefore, Friend! these Voices of the Earth--
  The rhythmic records of my life's career,
Humble, perhaps, yet wanting not the worth
  Of Truth, and to the heart of Nature near.
Take them, and your acceptance, in the dearth
  Of the world's tardy praise, shall make them dear.

POEMS OF THE ORIENT.

Da der West ward durchgekostet,
Hat er nun den Ost entmostet.

Rückert.

A PÆAN TO THE DAWN.

I.

THE dusky sky fades into blue,
  And bluer surges bind us;
The stars are glimmering faint and few,
  The night is left behind us!
Turn not where sinks the sullen dark
  Before the signs of warning,
But crowd the canvas on our bark
  And sail to meet the morning.
Rejoice! rejoice! the hues that fill
  The orient, flush and lighten;
And over the blue Ionian hill
  The Dawn begins to brighten!

II.

We leave the Night, that weighed so long
  Upon the soul's endeavor,
For Morning, on these hills of Song,
  Has made her home forever.
Hark to the sound of trump and lyre,
  In the olive groves before us,
And the rhythmic beat, the pulse of fire,
  Throb in the full-voiced chorus!
More than Memnonian grandeur speaks
  In the triumph of the pæan,
And all the glory of the Greeks
  Breathes o'er the old Ægean.

III.

Here shall the ancient Dawn return,
  That lit the earliest poet,
Whose very ashes in his urn
  Would radiate glory through it —
The dawn of Life, when Life was Song,
  And Song the life of Nature,

And the Singer stood amid the throng —
  A God in every feature!
When Love was free, and free as air
  The utterance of Passion,
And the heart in every fold lay bare,
  Nor shamed its true expression.

IV.

Then perfect limb and perfect face
  Surpassed our best ideal;
Unconscious Nature's law was grace —
  The Beautiful was real.
For men acknowledged true desires,
  And light as garlands wore them;
They were begot by vigorous sires,
  And noble mothers bore them.
O, when the shapes of Art they planned
  Were living forms of passion,
Impulse and Deed went hand in hand,
  And Life was more than Fashion!

V.

The seeds of Song they scattered first
  Flower in all later pages;

Their forms have woke the Artist's thirst
  Through the succeeding ages:
But I will seek the fountain-head
  Whence flowed their inspiration,
And lead the unshackled life they led,
  Accordant with Creation.
The World's false life, that follows still,
  Has ceased its chain to tighten,
And over the blue Ionian hill
  I see the sunrise brighten!

THE POET IN THE EAST.

THE Poet came to the Land of the East,
  When Spring was in the air :
The Earth was dressed for a wedding feast,
  So young she seemed, and fair ;
And the Poet knew the Land of the East —
  His soul was native there.

All things to him were the visible forms
  Of early and precious dreams —
Familiar visions that mocked his quest
  Beside the Western streams,
Or gleamed in the gold of the clouds, unrolled
  In the sunset's dying beams.

He looked above in the cloudless calm,
  And the Sun sat on his throne ;

The breath of gardens, deep in balm,
  Was all about him blown,
And a brother to him was the princely Palm,
  For he cannot live alone.

His feet went forth on the myrtled hills,
  And the flowers their welcome shed;
The meads of milk-white asphodel
  They knew the Poet's tread,
And far and wide, in a scarlet tide,
  The poppy's bonfire spread.

And, half in shade and half in sun,
  The Rose sat in her bower,
With a passionate thrill in her crimson heart —
  She had waited for the hour!
And, like a bride's, the Poet kissed
  The lips of the glorious flower.

Then the Nightingale, who sat above
  In the boughs of the citron tree,
Sang: We are no rivals, brother mine,
  Except in minstrelsy;
For the rose you kissed with the kiss of love
  Is faithful still to me.

And further sang the Nightingale :
  Your bower not distant lies.
I heard the sound of a Persian lute
  From the jasmined window rise,
And like two stars, through the lattice-bars,
  I saw the Sultana's eyes.

The Poet said : I will here abide,
  In the Sun's unclouded door ;
Here are the wells of all delight
  On the lost Arcadian shore :
Here is the light on sea and land,
  And the dream deceives no more.

THE TEMPTATION OF HASSAN BEN KHALED.

I.

HASSAN BEN KHALED, singing in the streets
Of Cairo, sang these verses at my door :
" Blessed is he, who God and Prophet greets
Each morn with prayer ; but he is blest much more
Whose conduct is his prayer's interpreter.
Sweeter than musk, and pleasanter than myrrh,
Richer than rubies, shall his portion be,
When God bids Azrael : 'bring him unto me!'
But woe to him whose life casts dirt upon
The Prophet's word ! When all his days are done,
Him shall the Evil Angel trample down
Out of the sight of God." Thus, with a frown
Of the severest virtue, Hassan sang
Unto the people, till the markets rang.

II.

But two days after this, he came again
And sang, and I remarked an altered strain.
Before my shop he stood, with forehead bent
Like one whose sin hath made him penitent —
In whom the pride, that like a stately reed
Lifted his head, is broken. "Blest, indeed,"
(These were his words,) "is he who never fell,
But blest much more, who from the verge of Hell
Climbs up to Paradise: for Sin is sweet;
Strong is Temptation; willing are the feet
That follow Pleasure, manifold her snares,
And pitfalls lurk beneath our very prayers:
Yet God, the Clement, the Compassionate,
In pity of our weakness keeps the gate
Of Pardon open, scorning not to wait
Till the last moment, when His mercy flings
A splendor from the shade of Azrael's wings."
"Wherefore, O Poet!" I to Hassan said,
"This altered measure? Wherefore hang your head,
O Hassan! whom the pride of virtue gives
The right to face the holiest man that lives?
Enter, I pray thee: this poor house will be
Honored henceforth, if it may shelter thee."

Hassan Ben Khaled lifted up his eyes
To mine, a moment: then, in cheerful guise,
He passed my threshold with unslippered feet.

III.

I led him from the noises of the street
To the cool inner chambers, where my slave
Poured out the pitcher's rosy-scented wave
Over his hands, and laid upon his knee
The napkin, silver-fringed: and when the pipe
Exhaled a grateful odor from the ripe
Latakian leaves, said Hassan unto me:
"Listen, O Man! no man can truly say
That he hath wisdom. What I sang to-day
Was not less truth than what I sang before,
But to Truth's house there is a single door,
Which is Experience. He teaches best,
Who feels the hearts of all men in his breast
And knows their strength or weakness through his own.
The holy pride, that never was o'erthrown,
Was never tempted, and its words of blame
Reach but the dull ears of the multitude:
The admonitions, fruitful unto good,
Come from the voice of him who conquers shame."

IV.

" Give me, O Poet! (if thy friend may be
Worthy such confidence,") I said ; " the key
Unto thy words, that I may share with thee
Thine added wisdom." Hassan's kindly eye
Before his lips unclosed, spake willingly,
And he began : " But two days since, I went
Singing what thou didst hear, with soul intent
On my own virtue, all the markets through ;
And when about the time of prayer, I drew
Near to the Gate of Victory, behold!
There came a man, whose turban fringed with gold
And golden cimeter, bespake his wealth :
' May God prolong thy days, O Hassan! Health
And Fortune be thy wisdom's aids!' he cried ;
' Come to my garden by the river's side,
Where other poets wait thee. Be my guest,
For even the Prophets had their times of rest,
And Rest, that strengthens unto virtuous deeds,
Is one with Prayer.' Two royal-blooded steeds,
Held by his grooms, were waiting at the gate,
And though I shrank from such unwonted state
The master's words were manna to my pride,
And, mounting straightway, forth we twain did ride
Unto the garden by the river's side.

V.

Never till then had I beheld such bloom.
The west wind sent its heralds of perfume
To bid us welcome, midway on the road.
Full in the sun the marble portal glowed
Like silver, but within the garden wall
No ray of sunshine found a place to fall,
So thick the crowning foliage of the trees,
Roofing the walks with twilight ; and the air
Under their tops was greener than the seas,
And cool as they. The forms that wandered there
Resembled those who populate the floor
Of Ocean, and the royal lineage own
That gave a Princess unto Persia's throne.
All fruits the trees of this fair garden bore,
Whose balmy fragrance lured the tongue to taste
Their flavors : there bananas flung to waste
Their golden flagons with thick honey filled ;
From splintered cups the ripe pomegranates spilled
A shower of rubies ; oranges that glow
Like globes of fire, enclosed a heart of snow
Which thawed not in their flame ; like balls of gold
The peaches seemed, that had in blood been rolled ;
Pure saffron mixed with clearest amber stained
The apricots ; bunches of amethyst

And sapphire seemed the grapes, so newly kissed
That still the mist of Beauty's breath remained,
And where the lotus slowly swung in air
Her snowy-bosomed chalice, rosy-veined,
The golden fruit swung softly-cradled there,
Even as a bell upon the bosom swings
Of some fair dancer — happy bell, that sings
For joy, its golden tinkle keeping time
To the heart's beating and the cymbal's chime!
There dates of agate and of jasper lay,
Dropped from the bounty of the pregnant palm,
And all ambrosial trees, all fruits of balm,
All flowers of precious odors, made the day
Sweet as a morn of Paradise. My breath
Failed with the rapture, and with doubtful mind
I turned to where the garden's lord reclined,
And asked, "Was not that gate the Gate of Death?"

VI.

The guests were near a fountain. As I came
They rose in welcome, wedding to my name
Titles of honor, linked in choicest phrase,
For Poets' ears are ever quick to Praise,
The 'Open Sesamè!' whose magic art
Forces the guarded entrance of the heart.

Young men were they, whose manly beauty made
Their words the sweeter, and their speech displayed
Knowledge of men, and of the Prophet's laws.
Pleasant our converse was, where every pause
Gave to the fountain leave to sing its song,
Suggesting further speech ; until, ere long,
There came a troop of swarthy slaves, who bore
Ewers and pitchers all of silver ore,
Wherein we washed our hands ; then, tables placed,
And brought us meats of every sumptuous taste
That makes the blood rich — pheasants stuffed with spice ;
Young lambs, whose entrails were of cloves and rice ;
Ducks bursting with pistachio nuts, and fish
That in a bed of parsley swam. Each dish,
Cooked with such art, seemed better than the last,
And our indulgence in the rich repast
Brought on the darkness ere we missed the day :
But lamps were lighted in the fountain's spray,
Or, pendent from the boughs, their colors told
What fruits unseen, of crimson or of gold,
Scented the gloom. Then took the generous host
A basket filled with roses. Every guest
Cried, " Give me roses ! " and he thus addressed
His words to all : " He who exalts them most
In song, he only shall the roses wear."

Then sang a guest: " The rose's cheeks are fair;
It crowns the purple bowl, and no one knows
If the rose colors it, or it the rose."
And sang another: " Crimson is its hue,
And on its breast the morning's crystal dew
Is changed to rubies." Then a third replied:
" It blushes in the sun's enamoured sight,
As a young virgin on her wedding night,
When from her face the bridegroom lifts the veil."
When all had sung their songs, I, Hassan, tried.
" The Rose," I sang, " is either red or pale,
Like maidens whom the flame of passion burns,
And Love or Jealousy controls, by turns.
Its buds are lips preparing for a kiss;
Its open flowers are like the blush of bliss
On lovers' cheeks; the thorns its armor are,
And in its centre shines a golden star,
As on a favorite's cheek a sequin glows —
And thus the garden's favorite is the Rose."

VII.

The master from his open basket shook
The roses on my head. The others took
Their silver cups, and filling them with wine,

Cried, " Pledge our singing, Hassan, as we thine!"
But I exclaimed, " What is it I have heard?
Wine is forbidden by the Prophet's word:
Surely, O Friends! ye would not lightly break
The laws which bring ye blessing?" Then they spake:
" O Poet, learn thou that the law was made
For men, and not for poets. Turn thine eye
Within, and read the nature there displayed;
The gifts thou hast doth Allah's grace deny
To common men; they lift thee o'er the rules
The Prophet fixed for sinners and for fools.
The vine is Nature's poet: from his bloom
The air goes reeling, tipsy with perfume,
And when the sun is warm within his blood
It mounts and sparkles in a crimson flood;
Rich with dumb songs he speaks not, till they find
Interpretation in the Poet's mind.
If Wine be evil, Song is evil too;
Then cease thy singing, lest it bring thee sin;
But wouldst thou know the strains which Hafiz knew,
Drink as he drank, and thus the secret win."
They clasped my glowing hands; they held the bowl
Up to my lips, till, losing all control
Of the fierce thirst, which at my scruples laughed,
I drained the goblet at a single draught.

It ran through every limb like fluid fire:
"More, O my Friends!" I cried, the new desire
Raging within me: "this is life indeed!
From blood like this is coined the nobler seed
Whence poets are begotten. Drink again,
And give us music of a tender strain,
Linking your inspiration unto mine,
For music hovers on the lips of Wine!"

VIII.

"Music!" they shouted, echoing my demand,
And answered with a beckon of his hand
The gracious host, whereat a maiden, fair
As the last star that leaves the morning air,
Came down the leafy paths. Her veil revealed
The beauty of her face, which, half concealed
Behind its thin blue folds, showed like the moon
Behind a cloud that will forsake it soon.
Her hair was braided darkness, but the glance
Of lightning eyes shot from her countenance,
And showed her neck, that like an ivory tower
Rose o'er the twin domes of her marble breast.
Were all the beauty of this age compressed
Into one form, she would transcend its power.

Her step was lighter than the young gazelle's,
And as she walked, her anklet's golden bells
Tinkled with pleasure, but were quickly mute
With jealousy, as from a case she drew
With snowy hands the pieces of her lute,
And took her seat before me. As it grew
To perfect shape, her lovely arms she bent
Around the neck of the sweet instrument,
Till from her soft caresses it awoke
To consciousness, and thus its rapture spoke:
"I was a tree within an Indian vale,
When first I heard the love-sick nightingale
Declare his passion: every leaf was stirred
With the melodious sorrow of the bird,
And when he ceased, the song remained with me.
Men came anon, and felled the harmless tree,
But from the memory of the songs I heard,
The spoiler saved me from the destiny
Whereby my brethren perished. O'er the sea
I came, and from its loud, tumultuous moan
I caught a soft and solemn undertone;
And when I grew beneath the maker's hand
To what thou seest, he sang (the while he planned)
The mirthful measures of a careless heart,
And of my soul his songs became a part.
Now they have laid my head upon a breast

Whiter than marble, I am wholly blest.
The fair hands smite me, and my strings complain
With such melodious cries, they smite again,
Until, with passion and with sorrow swayed,
My torment moves the bosom of the maid,
Who hears it speak her own. I am the voice
Whereby the lovers languish or rejoice;
And they caress me, knowing that my strain
Alone can speak the language of their pain."

IX.

Here ceased the fingers of the maid to stray
Over the strings; the sweet song died away
In mellow, drowsy murmurs, and the lute
Leaned on her fairest bosom, and was mute.
Better than wine that music was to me:
Not the lute only felt her hands, but she
Played on my heartstrings, till the sounds became
Incarnate in the pulses of my frame.
Speech left my tongue, and in my tears alone
Found utterance. With stretched arms I implored
Continuance, whereat her fingers poured
A tenderer music, answering the tone
Her parted lips released, the while her throat

Throbbed, as a heavenly bird were fluttering there,
And gave her voice the wonder of his note.
"His brow," she sang, "is white beneath his hair;
The fertile beard is soft upon his chin,
Shading the mouth that nestles warm within,
As a rose nestles in its leaves; I see
His eyes, but cannot tell what hue they be,
For the sharp eyelash, like a sabre, speaks
The martial law of Passion; in his cheeks
The quick blood mounts, and then as quickly goes,
Leaving a tint like marble when a rose
Is held beside it: — bid him veil his eyes,
Lest all my soul should unto mine arise,
And he behold it!" As she sang, her glance
Dwelt on my face; her beauty, like a lance,
Transfixed my heart. I melted into sighs,
Slain by the arrows of her beauteous eyes.
"Why is her bosom made" (I cried) "a snare?
Why does a single ringlet of her hair
Hold my heart captive?" "Would you know?"
she said;
"It is that you are mad with love, and chains
Were made for madmen." Then she raised her head
With answering love, that led to other strains,
Until the lute, which shared with her the smart,
Rocked as in storm upon her beating heart.

Thus to its wires she made impassioned cries:
"I swear it by the brightness of his eyes;
I swear it by the darkness of his hair;
By the warm bloom his limbs and bosom wear;
By the fresh pearls his rosy lips enclose;
By the calm majesty of his repose;
By smiles I coveted, and frowns I feared,
And by the shooting myrtles of his beard —
I swear it, that from him the morning drew
Its freshness, and the moon her silvery hue,
The sun his brightness, and the stars their fire,
And musk and camphor all their odorous breath:
And if he answer not my love's desire
Day will be night to me, and Life be Death!"

X.

Scarce had she ceased, when, overcome, I fell
Upon her bosom, where the lute no more
That night was cradled; song was silenced well
With kisses, each one sweeter than before,
Until their fiery dew so long was quaffed,
I drank delirium in the infectious draught.
The guests departed, but the sounds they made
I heard not; in the fountain-haunted shade

The lamps burned out; the moon rode far above,
But the trees chased her from our nest of love.
Dizzy with passion, in mine ears the blood
Tingled and hummed in a tumultuous flood,
Until from deep to deep I seemed to fall,
Like him, who from El Sirat's hair-drawn wall
Plunges to endless gulfs. In broken gleams
Glimmered the things I saw, so mixed with dreams
The vain confusion blinded every sense,
And knowledge left me. Then a sleep intense
Fell on my brain, and held me as the dead,
Until a sudden tumult smote my head,
And a strong glare, as when a torch is hurled
Before a sleeper's eyes, brought back the world.

XI.

Most wonderful! The fountain and the trees
Had disappeared, and in the place of these
I saw the well-known Gate of Victory.
The sun was high; the people looked at me,
And marvelled that a sleeper should be there
On the hot pavement, for the second prayer
Was called from all the minarets. I passed
My hand across my eyes, and found at last

What man I was. Then straightway through my heart
There ran a double pang — the bitter smart
Of evil knowledge, and the unhealthy lust
Of sinful pleasure ; and I threw the dust
Upon my head, the burial of my pride —
The ashen soil, wherein I plant the tree
Of Penitence. The people saw, and cried,
" May God reward thee, Hassan ! Truly, thou,
Whom men have honored, addest to thy brow
The crowning lustre of Humility :
As thou abasest, God exalteth thee ! "
Which when I heard, I shed such tears of shame
As might erase the record of my blame,
And from that time I have not dared to curse
The unrighteous, since the man who seemeth worse
Than I, may purer be ; for, when I fell,
Temptation reached a loftier pinnacle.
Therefore, O Man ! be Charity thy aim :
Praise cannot harm, but weigh thy words of blame.
Distrust the Virtue that itself exalts,
But turn to that which doth avow its faults,
And from Repentance plucks a wholesome fruit.
Pardon, not Wrath, is God's best attribute.

XII.

" The tale, O Poet! which thy lips have told,"
I said, " is words of rubies set in gold.
Precious the wisdom which from evil draws
Strength to fulfil the good, of Allah's laws.
But lift thy head, O Hassan! Thine own words
Shall best console thee, for my tongue affords
No phrase but thanks for what thou hast bestowed;
And yet I fain would have thee shake the load
Of shame from off thy shoulders, seeing still
That by this fall thou hast increased thy will
To do the work which makes thee truly blest."
Hassan Ben Khaled wept, and smote his breast:
"Hold! hold, O Man!" he cried: " why make me feel
A deeper shame? Must I to thee reveal
That Sin is as the leprous taint no art
Can cleanse the blood from? In my secret heart
I do believe I hold at dearer cost
The vanished Pleasure, than the Virtue lost."

So saying, he arose and went his way;
And Allah grant he go no more astray.

THE ARAB WARRIOR.

FROM THE ARABIC.

Go, ask of men that know my name,
  And they the truth will speak,
That I'm the terror of the strong,
  The helper of the weak.

My spear has made the dragon brood
  Succumb to galling bands,
And tossed before the jaws of War
  The forage he demands.

I steer my horse through stormy fights,
  As a seaman steers his craft;
My joy, to splinter on my breast
  The foeman's flying shaft.

40

I am the latest laid to rest,
The earliest in the fight,
And while the others idly feast
I rub my harness bright.

And while the booty they divide
I heap the ranks of slain,
And when they scorn my poverty,
I scorn their greed of gain.

ARAB PRAYER.

"*La illah il' Allah!*" the muezzin's call
Comes from the minaret, slim and tall,
That looks o'er the distant city's wall.

"*La illah il' Allah!*" the Faithful heed,
With God and the Prophet this hour to plead:
Whose ear is open to hear their need.

The sun is sunken; no vapor mars
The path of his going with dusky bars.
The silent Desert awaits the stars.

I bend the knee and I stretch the hand,
I strike my forehead upon the sand,
And I pray aloud, that He understand.

Not for my father, for he is dead ;
Not in my wandering brothers' stead —
For myself alone I bow the head.

God is Great, and God is Just :
He knoweth the hearts of the children of dust —
He is the Helper ; in Him I trust.

My sword is keen and my arm is strong
With the sense of unforgotten wrong,
And the hate that waits and watches long.

God, let me wait for year on year,
But let the hour at last appear,
When Vengeance makes my honor clear.

Once let me strike till he is slain ;
His blood will cleanse my sabre's stain,
And I shall stand erect again.

Till then, I wander to and fro,
Wide as the desert whirlwinds go,
And seek, by the sun and stars, my foe.

Better than Stamboul's courts of gold,
Whose harems the Georgian girls infold,
Whiter than snow, but not so cold ;

Better than Baghdad's garden bowers,
Or fountains that play among Persian flowers;
Better than all delights and powers,

The deed God's justice will abide—
The stern atonement, long denied,
That righteous Vengeance gives to Pride.

EL KHALIL.

I AM no chieftain, fit to lead
Where spears are hurled and warriors bleed;
No poet, in my chanted rhyme
To rouse the ghosts of ancient time;
No magian, with a subtle ken
To rule the thoughts of other men;
Yet far as sounds the Arab tongue
My name is known to old and young.

My form has lost its pliant grace,
There is no beauty in my face,
There is no cunning in my arm,
The Children of the Sun to charm;
Yet, where I go, my people's eyes
Are lighted with a glad surprise,
And in each tent a couch is free,
And by each fire a place, for me.

They watch me from the palms, and some
Proclaim my coming ere I come.
The children lift my hand to meet
The homage of their kisses sweet;
With manly warmth the men embrace,
The veiléd maidens seek my face,
And eyes, fresh kindled from the heart,
Keep loving watch when I depart.

On God, the Merciful, I call,
To shed His blessing over all:
I praise His name, for he is Great,
And Loving, and Compassionate;
And for the gift of love I give —
The breath of life whereby I live —
He gives me back, in overflow,
His children's love, where'er I go.

Deep sunk in sin the man must be
That has no friendly word for me.
I pass through tribes whose trade is death,
And not a sabre quits the sheath;
For, strong and cruel as they prove,
The sons of men are weak to Love.
The humblest gifts to them I bring;
Yet in their hearts I rule, a king.

ODE TO INDOLENCE.

I.

FIND me a bower, in silent dells embayed,
And trebly guarded from each wind that blows,
Where the blue noon o'erroofs the tranquil shade,
And poppies breathe an odor of repose;
Where never noises from the distant world
Disturb the happy calm of soul and sense,
But in thy haven every sail is furled,
Divinest Indolence!
There shall I summon all melodious measures,
And *feel* the hymns to thee, I *sing* to other Pleasures.

II.

Within thy realm the vexing tempests die
  That strip the leaves from Life's aspiring tree,
And fairer blossoms open in thy sky,
  To richer fruits maturing peacefully.
What is the clangor of Ambition's car
  To thine eternal silence? To thy rest,
  What are the stormy joys that shake the breast,
And Passion's cloud, that leaves the thunder-scar?
On brows that burn with Toil's relentless fever
Thy pitying hand is laid, and they have calm forever.

III.

Where thou dost sit, the shadow of Despair
  Fell never; Hate and Envy thence depart;
Turn from thy gate the baffled hounds of Care,
  And the great strength of slumber fills the heart.
Even Love himself, far exiled, in thy bower,
  From the bright paths of rapture which he trod,
  Folds up his wing: in Indian Song, the god
Was born beneath the sleepy lotus-flower.
The only fugitive escaped the riot,
His presence glorifies thy charmed elysian quiet.

IV.

Far from thee drift the shattered hulks of life;
But the wrecked spirit slumbers at thy feet,
And, harbored now from every wave of strife,
Feels the strong pulses of Existence beat.
There hears the heart its native language, free
From the world's clamor; with enlightened eyes
There doth the soul its features recognize,
And read its destiny!
The dark enigmas which perplexed the sense
Fade in the wisdom, born of Indolence.

V.

Yea, let men struggle, toil, exult, and win
The pigmy triumphs which they fret to wear;
But I will fly the curse of primal sin,
And in thy lap the peace of Eden share.
Serener than a star on Twilight's breast,
A sea-flower, deep below the tropic waves,
Or sparry foliage of the dædal caves,
My life shall blossom in thine arms of rest.
My breath grows calm; my weary eyelids close;
And the pursuing Fates have left me to repose.

SONG.

Daughter of Egypt, veil thine eyes!
I cannot bear their fire;
Nor will I touch with sacrifice
Those altars of Desire.
For they are flames that shun the day,
And their unholy light
Is fed from natures gone astray
In passion and in night.

The stars of Beauty and of Sin,
They burn amid the dark,
Like beacons that to ruin win
The fascinated bark.
Then veil their glow, lest I forswear
The hopes thou canst not crown,
And in the black waves of thy hair
My struggling manhood drown!

AMRAN'S WOOING.

I.

You ask, O Frank! how Love is born
Within these glowing climes of Morn,
Where envious veils conceal the charms
That tempt a Western lover's arms,
And how, without a voice or sound,
From heart to heart the path is found,
Since on the eye alone is flung
The burden of the silent tongue.
You hearken with a doubtful smile
Whene'er the wandering bards beguile
Our evening indolence with strains
Whose words gush molten through our veins —
The songs of Love, but half confessed,
Where Passion sobs on Sorrow's breast,
And mighty longings, tender fears,
Steep the strong heart in fire and tears.

The source of each accordant strain
Lies deeper than the Poet's brain.
First from the people's heart must spring
The passions which he learns to sing;
They are the wind, the harp is he,
To voice their fitful melody —
The language of their varying fate,
Their pride, grief, love, ambition, hate —
The talisman which holds inwrought
The touchstone of the listener's thought;
That penetrates each vain disguise,
And brings his secret to his eyes.
For, like a solitary bird
That hides among the boughs unheard
Until some mate, whose carol breaks,
Its own betraying song awakes,
So, to its echo in those lays,
The ardent heart itself betrays.
Crowned with a prophet's honor, stands
The Poet, on Arabian sands;
A chief, whose subjects love his thrall —
The sympathizing heart of all.

II.

Vaunt not your Western maids to me,
Whose charms to every gaze are free :
My love is selfish, and would share
Scarce with the sun, or general air,
The sight of beauty which has shone
Once for mine eyes, and mine alone.
Love likes concealment ; he can dress
With fancied grace the loveliness
That shrinks behind its virgin veil,
As hides the moon her forehead pale
Behind a cloud, yet leaves the air
Softer than if her orb were there.
And as the splendor of a star,
When sole in heaven, seems brighter far,
So shines the eye, Love's star and sun,
The brighter, that it shines alone.
The light from out its darkness sent
Is Passion's life and element ;
And when the heart is warm and young,
Let but that single ray be flung
Upon its surface, and the deep
Heaves from its unsuspecting sleep,
As heaves the ocean when its floor
Breaks over the volcano's core.

Who thinks if cheek or lip be fair?
Is not all beauty centred where
The soul looks out, the feelings move,
And Love his answer gives to love?
Look on the sun, and you will find
For other sights your eyes are blind.
Look — if the colder blood you share
Can give your heart the strength to dare —
In eyes of dark and tender fire:
What more can blinded love desire?

III.

I was a stripling, quick and bold,
And rich in pride as poor in gold,
When God's good will my journey bent
One day to Shekh Abdallah's tent.
My only treasure was a steed
Of Araby's most precious breed;
And whether 'twas in boastful whim
To show his mettled speed of limb,
Or that presumption, which, in sooth,
Becomes the careless brow of youth, —
Which takes the world as birds the air,
And moves in freedom every where, —

It matters not. But 'midst the tents
I rode in easy confidence,
Till to Abdallah's door I pressed
And made myself the old man's guest.
My "Peace be with you!" was returned
With the grave courtesy he learned
From age and long authority,
And in God's name he welcomed me.
The pipe replenished, with its stem
Of jasmine wood and amber gem,
Was at my lips and while I drew
The rosy-sweet, soft vapor through
In ringlets of dissolving blue,
Waiting his speech with reverence meet,
A woman's garments brushed my feet,
And first through boyish senses ran
The pulse of love which made me man.
The handmaid of her father's cheer,
With timid grace she glided near,
And, lightly dropping on her knee,
Held out a silver zerf to me,
Within whose cup the fragrance sent
From Yemen's sunburnt berries blent
With odors of the Persian rose.
That picture still in memory glows
With the same heat as then — the gush
Of fever, with its fiery flush

Startling my blood; and I can see —
As she this moment knelt to me —
The shrouded graces of her form;
The half-seen arm, so round and warm;
The little hand, whose tender veins
Branched through the henna's orange stains;
The head, in act of offering bent;
And through the parted veil, which lent
A charm for what it hid, the eye,
Gazelle-like, large, and dark, and shy,
That with a soft, sweet tremble shone
Beneath the fervor of my own,
Yet could not, would not, turn away
The fascination of its ray,
But half in pleasure, half in fright,
Grew unto mine, and builded bright
From heart to heart a bridge of light.

IV.

From the fond trouble of my look
The zerf within her fingers shook,
As with a start, like one who breaks
Some happy trance of thought, and wakes

Unto forgotten toil, she rose
And passed. I saw the curtains close
Behind her steps: the light was gone,
But in the dark my heart dreamed on.
Some random words — thanks ill expressed —
I to the stately Shekh addressed,
With the intelligence which he,
My host, could not demand of me;
How, wandering in the desert chase,
I spied from far his camping-place,
And Arab honor bade me halt
To break his bread and share his salt.
Thereto, fit reverence for his name,
The praise our speech is quick to frame,
Which, empty though it seem, was dear
To the old warrior's willing ear,
And led his thoughts, by many a track,
To deeds of ancient prowess back,
Until my love could safely hide
Beneath the covert of his pride.
And when his "Go with God!" was said,
Upon El-Azrek's back I sped
Into the desert, wide and far,
Beneath the silver evening-star,
And, fierce with passion, without heed
Urged o'er the sands my snorting steed,

As if those afrites, feared of man, —
Who watch the lonely caravan,
And, if a loiterer lags behind,
Efface its tracks with sudden wind,
Then fill the air with cheating cries,
And make false pictures to his eyes
Till the bewildered sufferer dies, —
Had breathed on me their demon breath,
And spurred me to the hunt of Death.

V.

Yet madness such as this was worth
All the cool wisdom of the earth,
And sweeter glowed its wild unrest
Than the old calm of brain and breast.
The image of that maiden beamed
Through all I saw, or thought, or dreamed,
Till she became, like Light or Air,
A part of life. And she shall share,
I vowed, my passion and my fate,
Or both shall fail me, soon or late,
In the vain effort to possess ;
For Life lives only in success.
I could not, in her father's sight,
Purchase the hand which was his right;

And well I knew how quick denied
The prayer would be to empty pride ;
But Heaven and Earth shall sooner move
Than bar the energy of Love.
The sinews of my life became
Obedient to that single aim,
And desperate deed and patient thought
Together in its service wrought.
Keen as a falcon, when his eye
In search of quarry reads the sky,
I stole unseen, at eventide,
Behind the well, upon whose side
The girls their jars of water leaned.
By one long, sandy hillock screened,
I watched the forms that went and came,
With eyes that sparkled with the flame
Up from my heart in flashes sent,
As one by one they came and went
Amid the sunset radiance cast
On the red sands : they came and passed,
And she, — thank God ! — she came at last !

VI.

Then, while her fair companion bound
The cord her pitcher's throat around,

And steadied with a careful hand
Its slow descent, upon the sand
At the Shekh's daughter's feet, I sped
A slender arrow, shaft and head
With breathing jasmine-flowers entwined,
And roses such as on the wind
Of evening with rich odors fan
The white kiosks of Ispahan.
A moment, fired with love and hope,
I stayed upon the yellow slope
El-Azrek's hoofs, to see her raise
Her startled eyes in sweet amaze —
To see her make the unconscious sign
Which recognized the gift as mine,
And place, before she turned to part,
The flowery barb against her heart.

VII.

Again the Shekh's divan I pressed:
The jasmine pipe was brought the guest,
And Mariam, lovelier than before,
Knelt with the steamy cup once more.
O bliss! within those eyes to see
A soul of love look out on me —

A fount of passion, which is *truth*
In the wild dialect of Youth —
Whose rich abundance is outpoured
Like worship at a shrine adored,
And on its rising deluge bears
The heart to raptures or despairs.
While from the cup the zerf contained
The foamy amber juice I drained,
A rosebud in the zerf expressed
The sweet confession of her breast.
One glance of glad intelligence,
And silently she glided thence.
"O Shekh!" I cried, as she withdrew,
(Short is the speech where hearts are true,)
"Thou hast a daughter: let me be
A shield to her, a sword to thee!"
Abdallah turned his steady eye
Full on my face, and made reply:
"It cannot be. The treasure sent
By God must not be idly spent.
Strong men there are, in service tried,
Who seek the maiden for a bride;
And shall I slight their worth and truth
To feed the passing flame of youth?"

VIII.

" No passing flame ! " my answer ran ;
" But love which is the life of man,
Warmed with his blood, fed by his breath,
And, when it fails him, leaves but Death.
O Shekh, I hoped not thy consent ;
But having tasted in thy tent
An Arab welcome, shared thy bread,
I come to warn thee I shall wed
Thy daughter, though her suitors be
As leaves upon the tamarind tree.
Guard her as thou mayst guard, I swear
No other bed than mine shall wear
Her virgin honors, and thy race
Through me shall keep its ancient place.
Thou'rt warned, and duty bids no more ;
For, when I next approach thy door,
Her child shall intercessor be
To build up peace 'twixt thee and me."
A little flushed my boyish brow ;
But calmly then I spake, as now.
The Shekh, with dignity that flung
Rebuke on my impetuous tongue,

Replied : " The young man's hopes are fair ;
The young man's blood would all things dare.
But age is wisdom, and can bring
Confusion on the soaring wing
Of reckless youth. Thy words are just,
But needless ; for I still can trust
A father's jealousy to shield
From robber grasp the gem concealed
Within his tent, till he may yield
To fitting hands the precious store.
Go, then, in peace ; but come no more."

IX.

My only sequin served to bribe
A cunning mother of the tribe
To Mariam's mind my plan to bring.
A feather of the wild dove's wing,
A lock of raven gloss and stain
Sheared from El-Azrek's flowing mane,
And that pale flower whose fragrant cup
Is closed until the moon comes up, —
But then a tenderer beauty holds
Than any flower the sun unfolds, —

Declared my purpose. Her reply
Let loose the winds of ecstasy:
Two roses and the moonlight flower
Told the acceptance, and the hour —
Two daily suns to waste their glow,
And then, at moonrise, bliss — or woe.

X.

El-Azrek now, on whom alone
The burden of our fate was thrown,
Claimed from my hands a double meed
Of careful training for the deed.
I gave him of my choicest store —
No guest was ever honored more.
With flesh of kid, with whitest bread,
And dates of Egypt was he fed;
The camel's heavy udders gave
Their frothy juice his thirst to lave:
A charger, groomed with better care,
The Sultan never rode to prayer.
My burning hope, my torturing fear,
I breathed in his sagacious ear;
Caressed him as a brother might,
Implored his utmost speed in flight,

Hung on his neck with many a vow,
And kissed the white star on his brow.
His large and lustrous eyeball sent
A look which made me confident,
As if in me some doubt he spied,
And met it with a human pride.
" Enough : I trust thee. 'Tis the hour,
And I have need of all thy power.
Without a wing, God gives thee wings,
And Fortune to thy forelock clings."

XI.

The yellow moon was rising large
Above the Desert's dusky marge,
And save the jackal's whining moan,
Or distant camel's gurgling groan,
And the lamenting monotone
Of winds that breathe their vain desire
And on the lonely sands expire,
A silent charm, a breathless spell,
Waited with me beside the well.
She is not there — not yet — but soon
A white robe glimmers in the moon.

Her little footsteps make no sound
On the soft sand ; and with a bound,
Where terror, doubt, and love unite
To blind her heart to all but flight,
Trembling, and panting, and oppressed,
She threw herself upon my breast.
By Allah ! like a bath of flame
The seething blood tumultuous came
From life's hot centre as I drew
Her mouth to mine : our spirits grew
Together in one long, long kiss —
One swooning, speechless pulse of bliss,
That, throbbing from the heart's core, met
In the united lips. O, yet
The eternal sweetness of that draught
Renews the thirst with which I quaffed
Love's virgin vintage : starry fire
Leapt from the twilights of desire,
And in the golden dawn of dreams
The space grew warm with radiant beams,
Which from that kiss streamed o'er a sea
Of rapture, in whose bosom we
Sank down, and sank eternally.

XII.

Now nerve thy limbs, El-Azrek! Fling
Thy head aloft, and like a wing
Spread on the wind thy cloudy mane!
The hunt is up: their stallions strain
The urgent shoulders close behind,
And the wide nostril drinks the wind.
But thou art, too, of Nedjid's breed,
My brother! and the falcon's speed
Slant down the storm's advancing line
Would laggard be if matched with thine.
Still leaping forward, whistling through
The moonlight-laden air, we flew;
And from the distance, threateningly,
Came the pursuer's eager cry.
Still forward, forward, stretched our flight
Through the long hours of middle night;
One after one the followers lagged,
And even my faithful Azrek flagged
Beneath his double burden, till
The streaks of dawn began to fill
The East, and, freshening in the race,
Their goaded horses gained apace.

I drew my dagger, cut the girth,
Tumbled my saddle to the earth,
And clasped with desperate energies
My stallion's side with iron knees ;
While Mariam, clinging to my breast,
The closer for that peril pressed.
They come ! they come ! Their shouts we hear,
Now faint and far, now fierce and near.
O brave El-Azrek ! on the track
Let not one fainting sinew slack,
Or know thine agony of flight
Endured in vain ! The purple light
Of breaking morn has come at last.
O joy ! the thirty leagues are past ;
And, gleaming in the sunrise, see
The white tents of the Aneyzee !
The warriors of the waste, the foes
Of Shekh Abdallah's tribe, are those
Whose shelter and support I claim,
Which they bestow in Allah's name ;
While, wheeling back, the baffled few
No longer ventured to pursue.

XIII.

And now, O Frank! if you would see
How soft the eyes that looked on me
Through Mariam's silky lashes, scan
Those of my little Solyman.
And should you marvel if the child
His stately grandsire reconciled
To that bold theft, when years had brought
The golden portion which he sought,
And what upon this theme befell,
The Shekh himself can better tell.

A PLEDGE TO HAFIZ.

Brim the bowls with Shiraz wine!
Roses round your temples twine;
Brim the bowls with Shiraz wine —
Hafiz pledge we, Bard divine!
With the summer warmth that glows
In the wine and on the rose,
Blushing, fervid, ruby-bright,
We shall pledge his name aright.

Hafiz, in whose measures move
Youth and Beauty, Song and Love —
In his veins the nimble flood
Was of wine, and not of blood.
All the songs he sang or thought
In his brain were never wrought,
But like rose leaves fell apart
From that bursting rose, his heart.

Youth is morning's transient ray;
Love consumes itself away;
Time destroys what Beauty gives;
But in Song the Poet lives.
While we pledge him — thus — and thus —
He is present here in us;
'Tis his voice that cries, not mine:
Brim the bowls with Shiraz wine!

THE GARDEN OF IREM.

HAVE you seen the Garden of Irem?
No mortal knoweth the road thereto.
Find me a path in the mists that gather
When the sunbeams scatter the morning dew,
And I will lead you thither.
Give me a key to the halls of the sun
When he goes behind the purple sea,
Or a wand to open the vaults that run
Down to the afrite-guarded treasures,
And I will open its doors to thee.
Who hath tasted its countless pleasures?
Who hath breathed, in its winds of spice,
Raptures deeper than Paradise?
Who hath trodden its ivory floors,
Where the fount drops pearl from a golden shell,
And heard the hinges of diamond doors
Swing to the music of Israfel?

Its roses blossom, its palms arise,
By the phantom stream that flows so fair
Under the Desert's burning skies.
Can you reach that flood, can you drink its tide,
Can you swim its waves to the farther side,
Your feet may enter there.

II.

I have seen the Garden of Irem.
I found it, but I sought it not:
Without a path, without a guide,
I found the enchanted spot:
Without a key its golden gate stood wide.
I was young, and strong, and bold, and free
As the milk-white foal of the Nedjidee,
And the blood in my veins was like sap of the vine,
That stirs, and mounts, and will not stop
Till the breathing blossoms that bring the wine
Have drained its balm to the last sweet drop.
Lance and barb were all I knew,
Till deep in the Desert the spot I found,
Where the marvellous gates of Irem threw
Their splendors over an unknown ground.
Mine were the pearl and ivory floors,
Mine the music of diamond doors,

Turning each on a newer glory:
Mine were the roses whose bloom outran
The spring-time beauty of Gulistan,
And the fabulous flowers of Persian story.
Mine were the palms of silver stems,
And blazing emerald for diadems;
The fretted arch and the gossamer wreath,
So light and frail you feared to breathe;
Yet o'er them rested the pendent spars
Of domes bespangled with silver stars,
And crusted gems of rare adorning:
And ever higher, like a shaft of fire,
The lessening links of the golden spire
Flamed in the myriad-colored morning!

Like one who lies on the marble lip
Of the blessed bath in a tranquil rest,
And stirs not even a finger's tip
Lest the beatific dream should slip,
So did I lie in Irem's breast.
Sweeter than Life and stronger than Death
Was every draught of that blissful breath;
Warmer than Summer came its glow
To the youthful heart in a mighty flood,
And sent its bold and generous blood
To water the world in its onward flow.

There, where the Garden of Irem lies,
Are the roots of the Tree of Paradise,
And happy are they who sit below,
When into this world of Strife and Death
The blossoms are shaken by Allah's breath.

THE BIRTH OF THE HORSE.

FROM THE ARABIC.

THE South Wind blows from Paradise —
A wind of fire and force ;
And yet his proudest merit is
That he begat the Horse.

When Allah's breath created first
The noble Arab steed, —
The conqueror of all his race
In courage and in speed, —

To the South Wind He spake : From thee
A creature shall have birth,
To be the bearer of my arms
And my renown on Earth.

The pride of all the Faithful, he —
 The terror of their foes:
Rider and Horse shall comrades be
 In battle and repose.

Then to the perfect Horse He spake:
 Fortune to thee I bring;
Fortune, as long as rolls the Earth,
 Shall to thy forelock cling.

Without a pinion winged thou art,
 And fleetest with thy load;
Bridled art thou without a rein,
 And spurred without a goad.

Men shall bestride thee who have made
 Their fame, their service, mine;
And, when they pray upon their way,
 Their prayers shall count as thine.

The worship which thy master speaks
 Thou sharest silently;
By mutual fate he rises up,
 Or falls to Earth with thee.

THE WISDOM OF ALI.

AN ARAB LEGEND.

THE Prophet once, sitting in calm debate,
Said: "I am Wisdom's fortress; but the gate
Thereof is Ali." Wherefore, some who heard,
With unbelieving jealousy were stirred;
And, that they might on him confusion bring,
Ten of the boldest joined to prove the thing.
"Let us in turn to Ali go," they said,
"And ask if Wisdom should be sought instead
Of earthly riches; then, if he reply
To each of us, in thought, accordantly,
And yet to none, in speech or phrase, the same,
His shall the honor be, and ours the shame."

Now, when the first his bold demand did make,
These were the words which Ali straightway spake:

" Wisdom is the inheritance of those
Whom Allah favors ; riches, of his foes."

Unto the second he said : " Thyself must be
Guard to thy wealth ; but Wisdom guardeth thee."

Unto the third : " By Wisdom wealth is won ;
But riches purchased wisdom yet for none."

Unto the fourth : " Thy goods the thief may take ;
But into Wisdom's house he cannot break."

Unto the fifth : " Thy goods decrease the more
Thou giv'st ; but use enlarges Wisdom's store."

Unto the sixth : " Wealth tempts to evil ways ;
But the desire of Wisdom is God's praise."

Unto the seventh : " Divide thy wealth, each part
Becomes a pittance. Give with open heart
Thy wisdom, and each separate gift shall be
All that thou hast, yet not impoverish thee."

Unto the eighth : " Wealth cannot keep itself ;
But Wisdom is the steward even of pelf."

Unto the ninth: "The camels slowly bring
Thy goods; but Wisdom has the swallow's wing."

And lastly, when the tenth did question make,
These were the ready words which Ali spake:—
"Wealth is a darkness which the soul should fear;
But Wisdom is the lamp that makes it clear."

Crimson with shame the questioners withdrew,
And they declared: "The Prophet's words were
true;
The mouth of Ali is the golden door
Of Wisdom."

When his friends to Ali bore
These words, he smiled and said: "And should they
ask
The same until my dying day, the task
Were easy; for the stream from Wisdom's well,
Which God supplies, is inexhaustible."

AN ORIENTAL IDYL.

A SILVER javelin which the hills
  Have hurled upon the plain below,
The fleetest of the Pharpar's rills,
  Beneath me shoots in flashing flow.

I hear the never-ending laugh
  Of jostling waves that come and go,
And suck the bubbling pipe, and quaff
  The sherbet cooled in mountain snow.

The flecks of sunshine gleam like stars
  Beneath the canopy of shade;
And in the distant, dim bazaars
  I scarcely hear the hum of trade.

No evil fear, no dream forlorn,
  Darkens my heaven of perfect blue;
My blood is tempered to the morn —
  My very heart is steeped in dew.

What Evil is I cannot tell;
  But half I guess what Joy may be;
And, as a pearl within its shell,
  The happy spirit sleeps in me.

I feel no more the pulse's strife, —
  The tides of Passion's ruddy sea, —
But live the sweet, unconscious life
  That breathes from yonder jasmine tree.

Upon the glittering pageantries
  Of gay Damascus streets I look
As idly as a babe that sees
  The painted pictures of a book.

Forgotten now are name and race;
  The Past is blotted from my brain,
For Memory sleeps, and will not trace
  The weary pages o'er again.

I only know the morning shines,
 And sweet the dewy morning air;
But does it play with tendrilled vines?
 Or does it lightly lift my hair?

Deep-sunken in the charmed repose,
 This ignorance is bliss extreme:
And whether I be Man, or Rose,
 O, pluck me not from out my dream!

THE ANGEL OF PATIENCE.

" Patience is the key of Content." — MAHOMET.

To cheer, to help us, children of the dust,
  More than one angel has Our Father given;
But one alone is faithful to her trust —
  The best, the brightest exile out of Heaven.

Her ways are not the ways of pleasantness;
  Her paths are not the lightsome paths of joy,
She walks with wrongs that cannot find redress,
  And dwells in mansions Time and Death destroy.

She waits until her stern precursor, Care,
  Has lodged on foreheads, open as the morn,
To plough his deep, besieging trenches there —
  The signs of struggles which the heart has borne.

But when the first cloud darkens in our sky,
And face to face with Life we stand alone,
Silent and swift, behold! she draweth nigh,
And mutely makes our sufferings her own.

Though with its bitterness the heart runs o'er,
No words the sweetness of her lips divide;
But when the eye looks up for light once more,
She turns the cloud and shows its golden side.

Unto rebellious souls, that, mad with Fate,
To question God's eternal justice dare,
She points above with looks that whisper, "Wait—
What seems confusion here is wisdom there."

To the vain challenges of doubt we send,
No answering comfort doth she minister;
Her face looks ever forward to the end,
And we, who see it not, are led by her.

She doth not chide, nor in reproachful guise
The griefs we cherish rudely thrust apart;
But in the light of her immortal eyes
Revives the manly courage of the heart.

Daughter of God! who walkest with us here,
  Who mak'st our every tribulation thine,
Such light hast thou in Earth's dim atmosphere,
  How must thy seat in Heaven exalted shine!

How fair thy presence by those living streams
  Where Sin and Sorrow from their troubling cease!
Where on thy brow the crown of amaranth gleams,
  And in thy hand the golden key of Peace!

BEDOUIN SONG.

FROM the Desert I come to thee
  On a stallion shod with fire;
And the winds are left behind
  In the speed of my desire.
Under thy window I stand,
  And the midnight hears my cry:
I love thee, I love but thee,
  With a love that shall not die
        Till the sun grows cold,
        And the stars are old,
        And the leaves of the Judgment
          Book unfold!

Look from thy window and see
  My passion and my pain;
I lie on the sands below,
  And I faint in thy disdain.

Let the night-winds touch thy brow
  With the heat of my burning sigh,
And melt thee to hear the vow
  Of a love that shall not die
    Till the sun grows cold,
    And the stars are old,
    And the leaves of the Judgment
      Book unfold!

My steps are nightly driven,
  By the fever in my breast,
To hear from thy lattice breathed
  The word that shall give me rest.
Open the door of thy heart,
  And open thy chamber door,
And my kisses shall teach thy lips
  The love that shall fade no more
    Till the sun grows cold,
    And the stars are old,
    And the leaves of the Judgment
      Book unfold!

DESERT HYMN TO THE SUN.

I.

Under the arches of the morning sky,
  Save in one heart, there beats no life of Man;
The yellow sand-hills bleak and trackless lie,
  And far behind them sleeps the caravan.
A silence, as before Creation, broods
Sublimely o'er the desert solitudes.

II.

A silence as if God in Heaven were still,
  And meditating some new wonder! Earth
And Air the solemn portent own, and thrill
  With awful prescience of the coming birth.
And Night withdraws, and on their silver cars
Wheel to remotest space the trembling Stars.

III.

See ! an increasing brightness, broad and fleet,
Breaks on the morning in a rosy flood,
As if He smiled to see His work complete,
And rested from it, and pronounced it good.
The sands lie still, and every wind is furled :
The Sun comes up, and looks upon the world.

IV.

Is there no burst of music to proclaim
The pomp and majesty of this new lord ? —
A golden trumpet in each beam of flame,
Startling the universe with grand accord ?
Must Earth be dumb beneath the splendors thrown
From his full orb to glorify her own ?

V.

No : with an answering splendor, more than sound
Instinct with gratulation, she adores.
With purple flame the porphyry hills are crowned,
And burn with gold the Desert's boundless floors ;
And the lone Man compels his haughty knee,
And, prostrate at thy footstool, worships thee.

VI.

Before the dreadful glory of thy face
  He veils his sight ; he fears the fiery rod
Which thou dost wield amid the brightening space,
  As if the sceptre of a visible god.
If not the shadow of God's lustre, thou
Art the one jewel flaming on His brow.

VII.

Art thou, O Sun, Vicegerent of His will,
  To make on Earth His presence manifest ?
By Him created, yet creator still,
  Great Nature draws her being from thy breast :
Where thou art, Life's innumerous pulses play ;
And where thou art not, Death and fell Decay.

VIII.

Wrap me within the mantle of thy beams,
  And feed my pulses with thy keenest fire !
Here, where thy full meridian deluge streams
  Across the Desert, let my blood aspire
To ripen in the vigor of thy blaze,
And catch a warmth to shine through darker days !

IX.

I am alone before thee : Lord of Light !
Begetter of the life of things that live !
Beget in me thy calm, self-balanced might ;
To me thine own immortal ardor give.
Yea, though, like her who gave to Jove her charms,
My being wither in thy fiery arms.

X.

Whence came thy splendors ? Heaven is filled with thee ;
The sky's blue walls are dazzling with thy train ;
Thou sitt'st alone in the Immensity,
And in thy lap the World grows young again.
Bathed in such brightness, drunken with the Day,
He deems the Dark forever passed away.

XI.

But thou dost sheathe thy trenchant sword, and lean
With tempered grandeur towards the western gate ;
Shedding thy glory with a brow serene,
And leaving heaven all golden with thy state :
Not as a king discrowned and overthrown,
But one who keeps, and shall reclaim, his own.

NILOTIC DRINKING-SONG.

I.

You may water your bays, brother-poets, with lays
That brighten the cup from the stream you doat on,
By the Schuylkill's side, or Cochituate's tide,
Or the crystal lymph of the mountain Croton:
(We may pledge from these
In our summer ease,
Nor even Anacreon's shade revile us—)
But I, from the flood
Of his own brown blood,
Will drink to the glory of ancient Nilus!

II.

Cloud never gave birth, nor cradle the Earth,
To river so grand and fair as this is:
Not the waves that roll us the gold of Pactolus,
Nor cool Cephissus, nor classic Ilissus.

The lily may dip
Her ivory lip
To kiss the ripples of clear Eurotas;
But the Nile brings balm
From the myrrh and palm,
And the ripe, voluptuous lips of the lotus.

III.

The waves that ride on his mighty tide
Were poured from the urns of unvisited mountains;
And their sweets of the South mingle cool in the mouth
With the freshness and sparkle of Northern fountains.
Again and again
The goblet we drain—
Diviner a stream never Nereid swam on:
For Isis and Orus
Have quaffed before us,
And Ganymede dipped it for Jupiter Ammon.

IV.

Its blessing he pours o'er his thirsty shores,
And floods the regions of Sleep and Silence,
When he makes oases in desert places,
And the plain is a sea, the hills are islands.

And had I the brave
Anacreon's stave,
And lips like the honeyed lips of Hylas,
I'd dip from his brink
My bacchanal drink,
And sing for the glory of ancient Nilus!

CAMADEVA.

THE sun, the moon, the mystic planets seven,
  Shone with a purer and serener flame,
And there was joy on Earth and joy in Heaven
    When Camadeva came.

The blossoms burst, like jewels of the air,
  Putting the colors of the morn to shame;
Breathing their odorous secrets every where
    When Camadeva came.

The birds, upon the tufted tamarind spray,
  Sat side by side and cooed in amorous blame,
The lion sheathed his claws and left his prey
    When Camadeva came.

The sea slept, pillowed on the happy shore ;
The mountain-peaks were bathed in rosy flame ;
The clouds went down the sky — to mount no more
When Camadeva came.

The hearts of all men brightened like the morn ;
The poet's harp then first deserved its fame,
For rapture sweeter than he sang was born
When Camadeva came.

All breathing life a newer spirit quaffed,
A second life, a bliss beyond a name,
And Death, half-conquered, dropped his idle shaft
When Camadeva came.

NUBIA.

A LAND of Dreams and Sleep — a poppied land!
With skies of endless calm above her head,
The drowsy warmth of summer noonday shed
Upon her hills, and silence stern and grand
Throughout her Desert's temple-burying sand.
Before her threshold, in their ancient place,
With closéd lips, and fixed, majestic face,
Noteless of Time, her dumb colossi stand.
O, pass them not with light, irreverent tread;
Respect the dream that builds her fallen throne,
And soothes her to oblivion of her woes.
Hush! for she does but sleep; she is not dead:
Action and Toil have made the world their own,
But she hath built an altar to Repose.

KILIMANDJARO.

I.

HAIL to thee, monarch of African mountains,
Remote, inaccessible, silent, and lone —
Who, from the heart of the tropical fervors,
Liftest to heaven thine alien snows,
Feeding forever the fountains that make thee
Father of Nile and Creator of Egypt!

II.

The years of the world are engraved on thy forehead;
Time's morning blushed red on thy first-fallen snows;
Yet lost in the wilderness, nameless, unnoted,
Of Man unbeholden, thou wert not till now.
Knowledge alone is the being of Nature,

Giving a soul to her manifold features,
Lighting through paths of the primitive darkness
The footsteps of Truth and the vision of Song.
Knowledge has born thee anew to Creation,
And long-baffled Time at thy baptism rejoices.
Take, then, a name, and be filled with existence,
Yea, be exultant in sovereign glory,
While from the hand of the wandering poet
Drops the first garland of song at thy feet.

III.

Floating alone, on the flood of thy making,
Through Africa's mystery, silence, and fire,
Lo! in my palm, like the Eastern enchanter,
I dip from the waters a magical mirror,
And thou art revealed to my purified vision.
I see thee, supreme in the midst of thy co-mates,
Standing alone 'twixt the Earth and the Heavens,
Heir of the Sunset and Herald of Morn.
Zone above zone, to thy shoulders of granite,
The climates of Earth are displayed, as an index,
Giving the scope of the Book of Creation.
There, in the gorges that widen, descending
From cloud and from cold into summer eternal,

Gather the threads of the ice-gendered fountains—
Gather to riotous torrents of crystal,
And, giving each shelvy recess where they dally
The blooms of the North and its evergreen turfage,
Leap to the land of the lion and lotus!
There, in the wondering airs of the Tropics
Shivers the Aspen, still dreaming of cold:
There stretches the Oak, from the loftiest ledges,
His arms to the far-away lands of his brothers,
And the Pine-tree looks down on his rival, the Palm.

IV.

Bathed in the tenderest purple of distance,
Tinted and shadowed by pencils of air,
Thy battlements hang o'er the slopes and the forests,
Seats of the Gods in the limitless ether,
Looming sublimely aloft and afar.
Above them, like folds of imperial ermine,
Sparkle the snow-fields that furrow thy forehead—
Desolate realms, inaccessible, silent,
Chasms and caverns where Day is a stranger,
Garners where storeth his treasures the Thunder,
The Lightning his falchion, his arrows the Hail!

V.

Sovereign Mountain, thy brothers give welcome:
They, the baptized and the crownéd of ages,
Watch-towers of Continents, altars of Earth,
Welcome thee now to their mighty assembly.
Mont Blanc, in the roar of his mad avalanches,
Hails thy accession; superb Orizaba,
Belted with beech and ensandalled with palm;
Chimborazo, the lord of the regions of noonday,—
Mingle their sounds in magnificent chorus
With greeting august from the Pillars of Heaven,
Who, in the urns of the Indian Ganges
Filter the snows of their sacred dominions,
Unmarked with a footprint, unseen but of God.

VI.

Lo! unto each is the seal of his lordship,
Nor questioned the right that his majesty giveth:
Each in his awful supremacy forces
Worship and reverence, wonder and joy.
Absolute all, yet in dignity varied,

None has a claim to the honors of story,
Or the superior splendors of song,
Greater than thou, in thy mystery mantled —
Thou, the sole monarch of African mountains,
Father of Nile and Creator of Egypt !

MIMOSA BLOOMS.

I BREATHE your perfume, blessed flowers;
  And looking out, the blue waves o'er,
From Cadiz and her snow-white towers,
  I see the Egyptian shore.

Grateful as joy that comes again
  With solace sweeter than erewhile,
Your balsam fills my heart, as then,
  Beside the palmy Nile.

Your golden dust is on the sands
  Where yet my transient footprint lies;
And in the heaven of brighter lands
  Your little stars arise.

Ye fringe with down the thorny stems ;
  Ye flood the year with balm and spice,
More precious than the plant that gems
  The dells of Paradise.

Pure as a sinless virgin's prayer,
  Sweet as a sleeping infant's breath,
Ye mingle with the solemn air
  Of old Repose and Death.

Ye bear the bliss of Spring to realms
  Where endless Summer rules the hours ;
Noon's fiery deluge ne'er o'erwhelms
  The morning of your flowers.

Types of a Faith whose odors free
  Gently the stress of Life beguile,
Long may ye bloom and breathe for me,
  Ye darlings of the Nile !

THE BIRTH OF THE PROPHET.

I.

Thrice three moons had waxed in heaven, thrice three moons had waned away,
Since Abdullah, faint and thirsty, on the Desert's bosom lay
In the fiery lap of Summer, the meridian of the day; —

II.

Since from out the sand upgushing, lo! a sudden fountain leapt;
Sweet as musk and clear as amber, to his parching lips it crept.
When he drank it straightway vanished, but his blood its virtue kept.

III.

Ere the morn his forehead's lustre, signet of the Proph-
et's line,
To the beauty of Amina had transferred its flame di-
vine :
Of the germ within her sleeping, such the consecrated
sign.

IV.

And with every moon that faded waxed the splendor
more and more,
Till Amina's beauty lightened through the matron veil
she wore,
And the tent was filled with glory, and of Heaven it
seemed the door.

V.

When her quickened womb its burden had matured,
and Life began
Struggling in its living prison, through the wide Crea-
tion ran
Premonitions of the coming of a God-appointed
man.

VI.

For the oracles of Nature recognize a Prophet's
birth —
Blossom of the tardy ages, crowning type of human
worth —
And by miracles and wonders he is welcomed to the
Earth.

VII.

Then the stars in heaven grew brighter, stooping down-
ward from their zones;
Wheeling round the towers of Mecca, sang the moon
in silver tones,
And the Kaaba's grisly idols trembled on their granite
thrones.

VIII.

Mighty arcs of rainbow splendor, pillared shafts of pur-
ple fire,
Split the sky and spanned the darkness, and with many
a golden spire,
Beacon-like, from all the mountains streamed the lam-
bent meteors higher.

IX.

But when first the breath of being to the sacred infant
came,
Paled the pomp of airy lustre, and the stars grew dim
with shame,
For the glory of his countenance outshone their feebler
flame.

X.

Over Nedjid's sands it lightened, unto Oman's coral
deep,
Startling all the gorgeous regions of the Orient from
sleep,
Till, a sun on night new-risen, it illumed the Indian
steep.

XI.

They who dwelt in Mecca's borders saw the distant
realms appear
All around the vast horizon, shining marvellous and
clear,
From the gardens of Damascus unto those of Bende-
meer.

XII.

From the colonnades of Tadmor to the hills of Hadra-
maut,
Ancient Araby was lighted, and her sands the splendor
caught,
Till the magic sweep of vision overtook the track of
Thought.

XIII.

Such on Earth the wondrous glory, but beyond the
sevenfold skies
God His mansions filled with gladness, and the seraphs
saw arise
Palaces of pearl and ruby from the founts of Para-
dise.

XIV.

As the surge of heavenly anthems shook the solemn
midnight air,
From the shrines of false religions came a wailing of
despair,
And the fires on Pagan altars were extinguished every
where.

XV.

'Mid the sounds of salutation, 'mid the splendor and the
balm,
Knelt the sacred child, proclaiming, with a brow of
heavenly calm :
"God is God; there is none other; I his chosen Prophet
am!"

TO THE NILE.

Mysterious Flood, — that through the silent sands
  Hast wandered, century on century,
Watering the length of green Egyptian lands,
      Which were not, but for thee, —

Art thou the keeper of that eldest lore,
  Written ere yet thy hieroglyphs began,
When dawned upon thy fresh, untrampled shore
      The earliest life of Man?

Thou guardest temple and vast pyramid,
  Where the gray Past records its ancient speech;
But in thine unrevealing breast lies hid
      What they refuse to teach.

All other streams with human joys and fears
  Run blended, o'er the plains of History:
Thou tak'st no note of Man; a thousand years
    Are as a day to thee.

Thou, from thine unknown sources to the sea,
  Art of the Human Race a type sublime;
And Ocean waits thee, as Eternity
    Waits for the stream of Time.

What were to thee the Osirian festivals?
  Or Memnon's music on the Theban plain?
The carnage, when Cambyses made thy halls
    Ruddy with royal slain?

Even then thou wast a God, and shrines were built
  For worship of thine own majestic flood;
For thee the incense burned — for thee was spilt
    The sacrificial blood.

And past the bannered pylons that arose
  Above thy palms, the pageantry and state,
Thy current flowed, calmly as now it flows,
    Unchangeable as Fate.

Thou givest blessing as a God might give,
  Whose being is his bounty : from the slime
Shaken from off thy skirts the nations live,
      Through all the years of Time.

In thy solemnity, thine awful calm,
  Thy grand indifference of Destiny,
My soul forgets its pain, and drinks the balm
      Which thou dost proffer me.

Thy godship is unquestioned still : I bring
  No doubtful worship to thy shrine supreme ;
But thus my homage as a chaplet fling,
      To float upon thy stream !

HASSAN TO HIS MARE.

Come, my beauty! come, my desert darling!
  On my shoulder lay thy glossy head!
Fear not, though the barley-sack be empty,
  Here's the half of Hassan's scanty bread.

Thou shalt have thy share of dates, my beauty!
  And thou know'st my water-skin is free:
Drink and welcome, for the wells are distant,
  And my strength and safety lie in thee.

Bend thy forehead now, to take my kisses!
  Lift in love thy dark and splendid eye:
Thou art glad when Hassan mounts the saddle —
  Thou art proud he owns thee: so am I.

Let the Sultan bring his boasted horses,
  Prancing with their diamond-studded reins;
They, my darling, shall not match thy fleetness
  When they course with thee the desert-plains!

Let the Sultan bring his famous horses,
  Let him bring his golden swords to me —
Bring his slaves, his eunuchs, and his harem;
  He would offer them in vain for thee.

We have seen Damascus, O my beauty!
  And the splendor of the Pashas there:
What's their pomp and riches? Why, I would not
  Take them for a handful of thy hair!

Khaled sings the praises of his mistress,
  And, because I've none, he pities me:
What care I if he should have a thousand,
  Fairer than the morning? *I* have thee.

He will find his passion growing cooler
  Should her glance on other suitors fall;
Thou wilt ne'er, my mistress and my darling,
  Fail to answer at thy master's call.

By and by some snow-white Nedjid stallion
  Shall to thee his spring-time ardor bring ;
And a foal, the fairest of the Desert,
  To thy milky dugs shall crouch and cling.

Then, when Khaled shows to me his children,
  I shall laugh, and bid him look at thine ;
Thou wilt neigh, and lovingly caress me,
  With thy glossy neck laid close to mine.

CHARMIAN.

I.

O Daughter of the Sun!
Who gave the keys of passion unto thee?
Who taught the powerful sorcery
Wherein my soul, too willing to be won,
Still feebly struggles to be free,
But more than half undone?
Within the mirror of thine eyes,
Full of the sleep of warm Egyptian skies, —
The sleep of lightning, bound in airy spell,
And deadlier, because invisible, —
I see the reflex of a feeling
Which was not, till I looked on thee:
A power, involved in mystery,
That shrinks, affrighted, from its own revealing.

II.

Thou sitt'st in stately indolence,
Too calm to feel a breath of passion start
The listless fibres of thy sense,
The fiery slumber of thy heart.
Thine eyes are wells of darkness, by the veil
Of languid lids half-sealed : the pale
And bloodless olive of thy face,
And the full, silent lips that wear
A ripe serenity of grace,
Are dark beneath the shadow of thy hair.
Not from the brow of templed Athor beams
Such tropic warmth along the path of dreams ;
Not from the lips of hornéd Isis flows
Such sweetness of repose !
For thou art Passion's self, a goddess too,
And aught but worship never knew ;
And thus thy glances, calm and sure,
Look for accustomed homage, and betray
No effort to assert thy sway :
Thou deem'st my fealty secure.

III.

O Sorceress! those looks unseal
The undisturbéd mysteries that press
Too deep in nature for the heart to feel
Their terror and their loveliness.
Thine eyes are torches that illume
On secret shrines their unforeboded fires,
And fill the vaults of silence and of gloom
With the unresting life of new desires.
I follow where their arrowy ray
Pierces the veil I would not tear away,
And with a dread, delicious awe behold
Another gate of life unfold,
Like the rapt neophyte who sees
Some march of grand Osirian mysteries.
The startled chambers I explore,
And every entrance open lies,
Forced by the magic thrill that runs before
Thy slowly-lifted eyes.
I tremble to the centre of my being
Thus to confess the spirit's poise o'erthrown,
And all its guiding virtues blown
Like leaves before the whirlwind's fury fleeing.

IV.

But see ! one memory rises in my soul,
And, beaming steadily and clear,
Scatters the lurid thunder-clouds that roll
Through Passion's sultry atmosphere.
An alchemy more potent borrow
For thy dark eyes, enticing Sorceress !
For on the casket of a sacred Sorrow
Their shafts fall powerless.
Nay, frown not, Athor, from thy mystic shrine :
Strong Goddess of Desire, I will not be
One of the myriad slaves thou callest thine,
To cast my manhood's crown of royalty
Before thy dangerous beauty : I am free !

THE SHEKH.

FROM THE ARABIC.

Not a single
Star is twinkling
Through the wilderness of cloud:
On the mountain,
In the darkness,
Stands the Shekh, and prays aloud: —

God, who kindlest aspiration,
Kindlest hope the heart within, —
God, who promisest Thy mercy,
Wiping out the debt of sin, —

God, protect me, in the darkness,
When the awful thunders roll:
Evil walks the world unsleeping,
Evil sleeps within my soul.

Keep my mind from every impulse
  Which from Thee may turn aside ;
Keep my heart from every passion
  By Thy breath unsanctified.

God, preserve me from a spirit
  Which Thy knowledge cannot claim ;
From a knee that bendeth never
  In the worship of thy name ;

From a heart whose every feeling
  Is not wholly vowed to Thee ;
From an eye that, through its weeping,
  Thy compassion cannot see ;

From a prayer that goes not upward,
  In the darkness and the fear,
From the soul's impassioned centre,
  Seeking access at Thy ear !

When the might of Evil threatens,
  Throw Thy shelter over me :
Let my spirit feel Thy presence,
  And my days be full of Thee !

SMYRNA.

THE "Ornament of Asia" and the "Crown
Of fair Ionia." Yea; but Asia stands
No more an empress, and Ionia's hands
Have lost their sceptre. Thou, majestic town,
Art as a diamond on a faded robe:
The freshness of thy beauty scatters yet
The radiance of that sun of Empire set,
Whose disc sublime illumed the ancient globe.
Thou sitt'st between the mountains and the sea;
The sea and mountains flatter thine array,
And fill thy courts with Grandeur, not Decay;
And Power, not Death, proclaims thy cypress tree.
Through thee, the sovereign symbols Nature lent
Her rise, make Asia's fall magnificent.

TO A PERSIAN BOY,

IN THE BAZAAR AT SMYRNA.

THE gorgeous blossoms of that magic tree
Beneath whose shade I sat a thousand nights,
Breathed from their opening petals all delights
Embalmed in spice of Orient Poesy,
When first, young Persian, I beheld thine eyes,
And felt the wonder of thy beauty grow
Within my brain, as some fair planet's glow
Deepens, and fills the summer evening skies.
From under thy dark lashes shone on me
The rich, voluptuous soul of Eastern land,
Impassioned, tender, calm, serenely sad —
Such as immortal Hafiz felt when he
Sang by the fountain-streams of Rocnabad,
Or in the bowers of blissful Samàrcand.

THE GOBLET.

I.

When Life his lusty course began,
And first I felt myself a man,
And Passion's unforeboded glow —
The thirst to feel, the will to know —
Gave courage, vigor, fervor, truth,
The glory of the heart of Youth,
And each awaking pulse was fleet
A livelier march of joy to beat,
Presaging in its budding hour
The ripening of the human flower,
There came, on some divine intent,
One whom the Lord of Life had sent,
And from his lips of wisdom fell
This fair and wondrous oracle : —

II.

Life's arching temple holds for thee
Solution quick, and radiant key
To many an early mystery;
And thou art eager to pursue,
Through many a dimly-lighted clew,
The hopes that turn thy blood to fire,
The phantoms of thy young desire:
Yet not to reckless haste is poured
The nectar of the generous lord,
Nor mirth nor giddy riot jar
The penetralia, high and far;
But steady hope, and passion pure,
And manly truth, the crown secure.

III.

Within that temple's secret heart,
In mystic silence shrined apart,
There is a goblet, on whose brim
All raptures of Creation swim.
No light that ever beamed in wine
Can match the glory of its shine,

Or lure with such a mighty art
The tidal flow of every heart.
But in its warm, bewildering blaze,
An ever-shifting magic plays,
And few who round the altar throng
Shall find the sweets for which they long.
Who, unto brutish life akin,
Comes to the goblet dark with sin,
And with a coarse hand grasps, for him
The splendor of the gold grows dim,
The gems are dirt, the liquor's flame
A maddening beverage of shame,
And into caverns shut from day
The hot inebriate reels away.

IV.

For each shall give the draught he drains
Its nectar pure, or poison stains;
From out his heart the flavor flows
That gives him fury, or repose :
And some shall drink a tasteless wave,
And some increase the thirst they lave;
And others loathe as soon as taste,
And others pour the tide to waste;

And some evoke from out its deeps
A torturing fiend that never sleeps —
For vain all arts to exorcise
From the seared heart its haunting eyes.

V.

But he who burns with pure desire,
With chastened love and sacred fire,
With soul and being all a-glow
Life's holiest mystery to know,
Shall see the goblet flash and gleam
As in the glory of a dream ;
And from its starry lip shall drink
A bliss to lift him on the brink
Of mighty rapture, joy intense,
That far outlives its subsidence.
The draught shall strike Life's narrow goal,
And make an outlet for his soul,
That down the ages, broad and far,
Shall brighten like a rising star.
In other forms his pulse shall beat,
His spirit walk in other feet,

And every generous hope and aim
That spurred him on to honest fame,
To other hearts give warmth and grace,
And keep on earth his honored place,
Become immortal in his race.

THE ARAB TO THE PALM.

NEXT to thee, O fair gazelle,
O Beddowee girl, beloved so well;

Next to the fearless Nedjidee,
Whose fleetness shall bear me again to thee;

Next to ye both I love the Palm,
With his leaves of beauty, his fruit of balm;

Next to ye both I love the Tree
Whose fluttering shadow wraps us three
With love, and silence, and mystery!

Our tribe is many, our poets vie
With any under the Arab sky;
Yet none can sing of the Palm but I.

The marble minarets that begem
Cairo's citadel-diadem
Are not so light as his slender stem.

He lifts his leaves in the sunbeam's glance
As the Almehs lift their arms in dance —

A slumberous motion, a passionate sign,
That works in the cells of the blood like wine.

Full of passion and sorrow is he,
Dreaming where the beloved may be.

And when the warm south-winds arise,
He breathes his longing in fervid sighs —

Quickening odors, kisses of balm,
That drop in the lap of his chosen palm.

The sun may flame and the sands may stir,
But the breath of his passion reaches her.

O Tree of Love, by that love of thine,
Teach me how I shall soften mine !

Give me the secret of the sun,
Whereby the wooed is ever won !

If I were a King, O stately Tree,
A likeness, glorious as might be,
In the court of my palace I'd build for thee!

With a shaft of silver, burnished bright,
And leaves of beryl and malachite;

With spikes of golden bloom a-blaze,
And fruits of topaz and chrysoprase:

And there the poets, in thy praise,
Should night and morning frame new lays —

New measures sung to tunes divine;
But none, O Palm, should equal mine!

AURUM POTABILE.

I.

BROTHER Bards of every region—
Brother Bards, (your name is Legion!)
Were you with me while the twilight
Darkens up my pine-tree skylight—
Were you gathered, representing
Every land beneath the sun,
O, what songs would be indited,
Ere the earliest star is lighted,
To the praise of vino d'oro,
On the Hills of Lebanon!

II.

Yes; while all alone I quaff its
Lucid gold, and brightly laugh its

Topaz waves and amber bubbles,
Still the thought my pleasure troubles,
        That I quaff it all alone.
Oh for Hafiz — glorious Persian!
Keats, with buoyant, gay diversion
Mocking Schiller's grave immersion;
        Oh for wreathed Anacreon!
Yet enough to have the living —
They, the few, the rapture-giving!
(Blessèd more than in receiving,)
Fate, that frowns when laurels wreathe them,
Once the solace might bequeath them,
Once to taste of vino d'oro,
        On the Hills of Lebanon!

III.

Lebanon, thou mount of story,
Well we know thy sturdy glory,
        Since the days of Solomon;
Well we know the Five old Cedars,
Scarred by ages — silent pleaders,
Preaching, in their gray sedateness,
Of thy forest's fallen greatness,

Of the vessels of the Tyrian,
And the palaces Assyrian,
And the temple on Morian
        To the High and Holy One!
Know the wealth of thy appointment—
Myrrh and aloes, gum and ointment;
But we knew not, till we clomb thee,
Of the nectar dropping from thee—
Of the pure, pellucid Ophir
In the cups of vino d'oro,
        On the Hills of Lebanon!

IV.

We have drunk, and we have eaten,
Where Egyptian sheaves are beaten;
Tasted Judah's milk and honey
On his mountains, bare and sunny;
Drained ambrosial bowls, that ask us
Never more to leave Damascus;
And have sung a vintage pæan
To the grapes of isles Ægean,
And the flasks of Orvieto,
        Ripened in the Roman sun:

But the liquor here surpasses
All that beams in earthly glasses.
'Tis of this that Paracelsus
(His elixir vitæ) tells us,
That to happier shores can float us
Than Lethean stems of lotus,
And the vigor of the morning
        Straight restores when day is done.
Then, before the sunset waneth,
While the rosy tide, that staineth
Earth, and sky, and sea, remaineth,
We will take the fortune proffered —
Ne'er again to be reoffered —
We will drink of vino d'oro,
        On the Hills of Lebanon!
Vino d'oro! vino d'oro! —
        Golden blood of Lebanon!

ON THE SEA.

THE pathway of the sinking moon
Fades from the silent bay;
The mountain-isles loom large and faint,
Folded in shadows gray,
And the lights of land are setting stars
That soon will pass away.

O boatman, cease thy mellow song!
O minstrel, drop thy lyre!
Let us hear the voice of the midnight sea,
Let us speak as the waves inspire,
While the plashy dip of the languid oar
Is a furrow of silver fire.

Day cannot make thee half so fair,
Nor the stars of eve so dear:

The arms that clasp and the breast that keeps,
    They tell me thou art near,
And the perfect beauty of thy face
    In thy murmured words I hear.

The lights of land have dropped below
    The vast and glimmering sea;
The world we leave is a tale that is told,—
    A fable, that cannot be.
There is no life in the sphery dark
    But the love in thee and me!

TYRE.

I.

The wild and windy morning is lit with lurid fire;
The thundering surf of ocean beats on the rocks of
Tyre —
Beats on the fallen columns and round the headland
roars,
And hurls its foamy volume along the hollow shores,
And calls with hungry clamor, that speaks its long de-
sire:
"Where are the ships of Tarshish, the mighty ships of
Tyre?"

II.

Within her cunning harbor, choked with invading sand,
No galleys bring their freightage, the spoils of every land,

And like a prostrate forest, when autumn gales have
blown,
Her colonnades of granite lie shattered and o'erthrown;
And from the reef the pharos no longer flings its fire
To beacon home from Tarshish the lordly ships of Tyre.

III.

Where is thy rod of empire, once mighty on the
waves —
Thou that thyself exalted, till Kings became thy slaves?
Thou that didst speak to nations, and saw thy will
obeyed —
Whose favor made them joyful, whose anger sore
afraid —
Who laid'st thy deep foundations, and thought them
strong and sure,
And boasted midst the waters: shall I not aye endure?

IV.

Where is the wealth of ages that heaped thy princely
mart?
The pomp of purple trappings; the gems of Syrian art;

The silken goats of Kedar; Sabæa's spicy store;
The tributes of the islands thy squadrons homeward bore,
When in thy gates triumphant they entered from the sea
With sound of horn and sackbut, of harp and psaltery?

V.

Howl, howl, ye ships of Tarshish! the glory is laid waste:
There is no habitation; the mansions are defaced.
No mariners of Sidon unfurl your mighty sails;
No workmen fell the fir-trees that grow in Shenir's vales,
And Bashan's oaks that boasted a thousand years of sun,
Or hew the masts of cedar on frosty Lebanon.

VI.

Rise, thou forgotten harlot! take up thy harp and sing:
Call the rebellious islands to own their ancient king:

Bare to the spray thy bosom, and with thy hair un-
bound,
Sit on the piles of ruin, thou throneless and discrowned!
There mix thy voice of wailing with the thunders of the
sea,
And sing thy songs of sorrow, that thou remembered
be!

VII.

Though silent and forgotten, yet Nature still laments
The pomp and power departed, the lost magnificence:
The hills were proud to see thee, and they are sadder
now;
The sea was proud to bear thee, and wears a troubled
brow,
And evermore the surges chant forth their vain desire:
"Where are the ships of Tarshish, the mighty ships of
Tyre?"

AN ANSWER.

You call me cold: you wonder why
  The marble of a mien like mine
Gives fiery sparks of Poesy,
  Or softens at Love's touch divine.

Go, look on Nature, you will find
  It is the rock that feels the sun:
But you are blind — and to the blind
  The touch of ice and fire is one.

REQUIEM IN THE SOUTH.

Thou hast no charm to turn the edge of Sorrow,
Bird of the mournful strain!
From thee doth Love a love more fervent borrow,
But Pain a sharper pain.

Why sing so loud, the passion-dream recalling,
That ceased in sudden gloom?
Why sing from boughs, whose ripened bloom is falling
Upon a maiden's tomb?

There needs no prompter for the love, belonging
To that sweet memory;
The heart's wild outcry, not its perished longing,
Demands a voice from thee.

The blackness of a grief that will not soften
Clings round me through the day,
And to the grave that hides her, wandering often,
I weep the nights away.

In this fierce sorrow there is no partaker—
It seeks no healing balm :
Yet, though my lamentations cannot wake her,
The exhausted heart grows calm.

Here, filled with sorrows of its own creation,
The night-wind swells and dies;
And, drooping in their dumb commiseration,
The palms around me rise.

Here, from the fury of my passion fleeing,
The barriers slowly fret,
Which dam the restless river of my being
To stagnate in regret.

And I may conquer this o'ermastering anguish,
And find my peace again ;
The manly heart must sometime cease to languish,
Ruled by the manly brain.

And what is wax shall be as steel within me,
        And be my fortune then :
All soft indulgence powerless to win me
        From the stern ways of men.

And let them say : " His heart is cold and cruel,
        He knows not love's desire : "
I gave the essence of my life as fuel
        To one extinguished fire.

GULISTAN.

AN ARABIC METRE.

Where is Gulistan, the Land of Roses?
Not on hills where Northern winters
Break their spears in icy splinters,
And in shrouded snow the world reposes;
But amid the glow and splendor
Which the Orient summers lend her,
Blue the heaven above her beauty closes:
There is Gulistan, the Land of Roses.

Northward stand the Persian mountains;
Southward spring the silver fountains
Which to Hafiz taught his sweetest measures,
Clearly ringing to the singing
Which the nightingales delight in,
When the Spring, from Oman winging
Unto Shiraz, showers her fragrant treasures
On the land, till valleys brighten,

Mountains lighten with returning
Fires of scarlet poppy burning,
And the stream meanders
Through its roseate oleanders,
And Love's golden gate, unfolden,
Opens on a universe of pleasures.

There the sunshine blazes over
Meadows gemmed with ruby clover;
There the rose's heart uncloses,
Prodigal with hoarded stores of sweetness,
And the lily's cup so still is
Where the river's waters quiver,
That no wandering air can spill his
Honeyed balm, or blight his beauty's fleetness.
Skies are fairest, days are rarest —
Thou, O Earth! a glory wearest
From the ecstasy thou bearest,
Once to feel the Summer's full completeness.

Twilight glances, moonlit dances,
Song by starlight, there entrances
Youthful hearts with fervid fancies,
And the blushing rose of Love uncloses:
Love that, lapped in summer joyance,
Far from every rude annoyance,
Calmly on the answering love reposes;

And in song, in music only
Speaks the longing, vague and lonely,
Which to pain is there the nearest,
Yet of joys the sweetest, dearest,
As a cloud when skies are clearest
On its folds intenser light discloses :
This is Gulistan, the Land of Roses.

JERUSALEM.

FAIR shines the moon, Jerusalem,
Upon the hills that wore
Thy glory once, their diadem
Ere Judah's reign was o'er:
The stars on hallowed Olivet
And over Zion burn,
But when shall rise thy splendor set?
Thy majesty return?

The peaceful shades that wrap thee now
Thy desolation hide;
The moonlit beauty of thy brow
Restores thine ancient pride;
Yet there, where Rome thy Temple rent,
The dews of midnight wet
The marble dome of Omar's tent,
And Aksa's minaret.

Thy strength, Jerusalem, is o'er,
And broken are thy walls ;
The harp of Israel sounds no more
In thy deserted halls :
But where thy Kings and Prophets trod,
Triumphant over Death
Behold the living Soul of God —
The Christ of Nazareth !

The halo of his presence fills
Thy courts, thy ways of men ;
His footsteps on thy holy hills
Are beautiful as then ;
The prayer, whose bloody sweat betrayed
His human agony,
Still haunts the awful olive shade
Of old Gethsemane.

Woe unto thee, Jerusalem !
Slayer of Prophets, thou,
That in thy fury stonest them
God sent, and sends thee now : —
Where thou, O Christ ! with anguish spent,
Forgave thy foes, and died,
Thy garments yet are daily rent —
Thy soul is crucified !

They darken with the Christian name
  The light that from thee beamed,
And by the hatred they proclaim
  Thy spirit is blasphemed;
Unto thine ear the prayers they send
  Were fit for Belial's reign,
And Moslem cimeters defend
  The temple they profane.

Who shall rebuild Jerusalem? —
  Her scattered children bring
From Earth's far ends, and gather them
  Beneath her sheltering wing?
For Judah's sceptre broken lies,
  And from his kingly stem
No new Messiah shall arise
  For lost Jerusalem!

But let the wild ass on her hills
  Its foal unfrighted lead,
And by the source of Kedron's rills
  The desert adder breed:
For where the love of Christ has made
  Its mansion in the heart,
He builds in pomp that will not fade
  Her heavenly counterpart.

How long, O Christ, shall men obscure
  Thy holy charity —
How long the godless rites endure,
  Which they bestow on thee?
Thou, in whose soul of tenderness
  The Father's mercy shone,
Who came, the sons of men to bless
  By Truth and Love alone.

The suns of eighteen hundred years
  Have seen thy reign expand,
And Morning, on her pathway, hears
  Thy name in every land;
But where thy sacred steps were sent
  The Father's will to bide,
Thy garments yet are daily rent —
  Thy soul is crucified!

THE VOYAGE OF A DREAM.

There is a cloud below the mountain peak,
Moored in the pauses of the uncertain air.
Its fleecy folds piled idly, self-involved,
Fashion the semblance of a floating throne,
Torn, in the clash of airy anarchy,
From the halls of Thunder; haply, once surcharged
With elemental fire and threatening death—
Fit seat for the Destroying Gods!—but now
Of ivory all compact, and touched with gold
And opal radiance on its sunny hem,
As if a peaceful Angel steered it down
From empyreal heights, with folded wing
Slow sinking through the yielding deeps. A throne
It seems, where disembodied Thought may sit,
Unquestioned take the sceptre of the world,
And, exercising power anticipant,
Go forth to try his lordship.

I accept
The moment's offer, mount the seat sublime,
And on the winds whose wings I feel no more,
Because I move before them, boldly try
The blue abyss whose measure no man knows.
Straight down the mountain sinks ; the mountain pines
Send a last drowning murmur faintly up
The ingulfing air, then stand in moveless calm,
Like coral forests rooted on the floors
Of Ocean. Plummeted with all her sins,
The Earth, down-sliding through the limpid sea,
Bears far below, the noises of her broils —
The greeds, the struggles, the devouring cares,
The endless agitations — leaving free
To the enfranchised spirit the still fields
Of amplest ether. Speed, my wingéd throne !
Wherever Thought may pilot, stretch thy flight,
Higher than eagle dares, above the peaks
Of Himalayan snow, o'er seas and sands,
Through tropic green, or where the eternal ice
Stiffens around the forehead of the Pole !
The World is mine ; the secrets of her heart
Lie at my feet ; she cannot shut them out :
And as she spins on her appointed round
From daylight into dark, from dark to dawn,
The mysteries of ages, problems which

A hundred centuries have left unsolved,
Give one by one their answers. Yonder burst
From the hot heart of Africa the springs
Of waters that have rocked Egyptian gods,
When the great stream that leaped in thunder down
From Primnis and Syene's barrier, bore
The chaplets and the consecrated oil
To his own godship poured : — Beyond those hills,
Whose tops against the Indian Caucasus
Uplift their snowy helms, behold the vast
Wind-driven platforms, whence the earliest Men
Went with the streams to greener pasture-fields,
And bore — their only heritage — God's name,
The altars of his worship, and the truths
Whose rude foundations underlie the piles
Of states and sovereignties, upholding firm
The masonry of Time : and whatsoe'er
Of summer beauty in the virgin isles,
Of lifeless grandeur in the emerald crags
Of undissolving ice, was never yet
By bold Adventure wrested from the keep
Of savage Nature, gives its secret up,
Helpless beneath the master-gaze of Thought,
As that of God.

Sweep downward, streams of air !
And thou, my cloudy chariot, drop thy shade

To roll, like dust, behind thy silent wheels,
And draw round Earth the triumph of our march!
See where, from zone to zone, the shadow moves —
A spot upon the Desert's golden glare —
A deeper blue on the far-stretching plains
Of Ocean's foamy azure — pausing now
To cloak with purple gloom the shoulders bare
Of mighty mountains, or ingulfed and lost
Deep in their folded chasms, or sailing slow
On wide savannas, the elysian home
Of flowery life, or quenching splendors vain
That dance upon the gilded domes of men,
And blind their eyes to the great light of Heaven.
As in this rarer ether I surmount
Life's numberless obstructions, and my gaze
Takes in the whole expanded round of Earth,
So, lifted o'er the narrow walks of Time,
The weary years have dwindled to a point,
And all their lessons compassed in the sphere
Of one sole thought, as in the dew-drop lies
The large orb of the morning sun. The years —
The ages, that from their accretion grow —
The cyclic eras — shrink, and all the Past
Lies round and clear beneath me, swallowing up
In one grand circumspect the separate lives,
The individual links whereby our hearts

Walk slowly back the difficult paths of Time,
Or climb some lesser eminence, to gain
A forward look that dimly penetrates
The nearest Future. Past and Future now
Unite their worlds in equal counterpoise,
And, effortless as dreams, the wisdom comes
That reads the hidden issues of all life,
The purpose of Creation.

Mount no more,
Thou flying cloud, but rather turn to dew
And weep thyself upon the clover meads,
And mix thy being with their honeyed bloom,
Than float alone within the highest vault
Of blue-cold ether, to dissolve alone
Into the thin, unfriendly air. Come down!
Come down! and let me quit this perilous height,
This icy royalty of thought, to glide
Nearer the homes of men, the embowered nests
Of unaspiring, lowliest content,
And joy, that from the beams of many hearts
Gathers its radiant focus, like a star
In the warm mists of Earth: nor yet enough
To glide above, but drop me in the fields
Or in the vales at evening, when from work
Accomplished, rest the glowing limbs of Toil,

And men have time to love — and I will kiss
The rugged cheek of Earth, with thankful tears
For every throb of every human heart
That welcomes me to share the general law,
And bear the mutual burden. Man alone
Creates Elysium for the soul of man.
The ample Future, and the godlike reach
Of new existence, are the prophecies
Of humblest Love, and in the souls that love
And are beloved the shining ether swims,
Whereon exalted, we o'erlook the world,
And Life, and Death, and every thing but Heaven.

L'ENVOI.

Unto the Desert and the desert steed
  Farewell! The journey is completed now:
Struck are the tents of Ishmael's wandering breed,
  And I unwind the turban from my brow.

The sun has ceased to shine; the palms that bent,
  Inebriate with light, have disappeared;
And naught is left me of the Orient
  But the tanned bosom and the unshorn beard.

Yet from that life my blood a glow retains,
  As the red sunshine in the ruby glows;
These songs are echoes of its fiercer strains —
  Dreams, that recall its passion and repose.

I found, among those Children of the Sun,
  The cipher of my nature — the release
Of baffled powers, which else had never won
  That free fulfilment, whose reward is peace.

For not to any race or any clime
  Is the completed sphere of life revealed;
He who would make his own that round sublime,
  Must pitch his tent on many a distant field.

Upon his home a dawning lustre beams,
  But through the world he walks to open day,
Gathering from every land the prismal gleams,
  Which, when united, form the perfect ray.

Go, therefore, Songs! — which in the East were born
  And drew your nurture — from your sire's control:
Haply to wander through the West forlorn,
  Or find a shelter in some Orient soul.

And if the temper of our colder sky
  Less warmth of passion and of speech demands,
They are the blossoms of my life — and I
  Have ripened in the suns of many lands.

II.

HYMN TO AIR.

I.

THE mightiest thou, among the Powers of Earth,
  The viewless Agent of the unseen God,
What immemorial era saw thy birth?
  What pathless fields of new Creation trod
Thy noiseless feet? Where was thy dwelling-place
  In the blind realm of Chaos, ere the word
  Of Sovereign Order by the stars was heard,
Or the young planet knew her Maker's face?
No wrecks are hid in thine unfathomed sea;
  Thy crystal tablets no inscription bear;
The awful Infinite is shrined in thee,
          Immeasurable Air!

II.

Thou art the Soul wherein the Earth renews
  The nobler life, that heals her primal scars;
Thine is the mantle of all-glorious hues,
  Which makes her beautiful among the stars;
Thine is the essence that informs her frame
  With manifold existence, thine the wing
  From gulfs of outer darkness sheltering,
And from the Sun's uplifted sword of flame.
She sleeps in thy protection, lives in thee;
  Thou mak'st the foreheads of her mountains smile;
His heart to thine, the all-surrounding Sea
  Spreads thy blue drapery o'er his cradled isle.
Thou art the breath of Nature, and the tongue
  Unto her dumb material being granted,
  And by thy voice her sorrowing psalms are chanted —
      Her hymns of triumph sung!

III.

Thine azure fountains nourish all that lives;
  Forever drained, yet ever brimming o'er,

Their billows in eternal freshness pour,
And from her choicest treasury Nature gives
A glad repayment of the debt she owes,
Replenishing thy sources : — balmy dews,
That on thy breast their summer tears diffuse ;
Strength from the pine, and sweetness from the rose ;
The spice of gorgeous Ind, the scents that fill
Ambrosial forests in the isles of palm ;
Leagues of perennial bloom on every hill ;
Lily and lotus in the water's calm ;
And where the torrent leaps to take thy wing,
But dashes out its life in diamond spray,
Or multitudinous waves of ocean fling
Their briny strength along thy rapid way —
Escapes some virtue which from thee they hold :
And even the grosser exhalations, fed
From Earth's decay, Time's crowded charnel-bed,
Fused in thy vast alembic, turn to gold.

IV.

Man is thy nursling, universal Air !
No kinder parent fosters him than thou :
How soft thy fingers dally with his hair !
How sweet their pressure on his fevered brow !

In the dark lanes where squalid Misery dwells,
  Where the fresh glories of existence shun
The childhood nurtured in the city's hells,
  And eyes that never saw the morning sun,
Pale cheeks for thee are pining, heavy sighs
Drawn from the depth of weary hearts, arise —
The flower of Life is withered on its stem,
  And the black shade the loathsome walls enclose
  Day after day more drear and stifling grows,
Till Heaven itself seems forfeited to them!
What marvel, then, as from a fevered dream
  The dying wakes, to feel his forehead fanned
By thy celestial freshness, he should deem
  The death-sweat dried beneath an angel's hand?
That tokens of the violet-sprinkled sod,
  Breathed like a blessing o'er his closing eyes,
  Should promise him the peace of Paradise —
    The pardon of his God?

V.

What is the scenery of Earth to thine?
  Here all is fixed in everlasting shapes,
But where the realms of gorgeous Cloudland shine,
  There stretch afar thy sun-illumined capes,

Embaying reaches of the amber seas
  Of sunset, on whose tranquil bosom lie
  The happy islands of the upper sky,
The halcyon shores of thine Atlantides.
Anon the airy headlands change, and drift
  Into sublimer forms, that slowly heave
  Their toppling masses up the front of eve,
Crag heaped on crag, with many a fiery rift,
And hoary summits, throned beyond the reach
  Of Alp or Caucasus: again they change,
  And down the vast, interminable range
Of towers and palaces, transcending each
The workmanship of Fable-Land, we see
  The "crystal, hyaline" of Heaven's own floor —
The radiance of the far Eternity
      Reflected on thy shore!

VI.

To the pure calm of thy cerulean deeps
  The jar of earth-born tumult cannot climb;
There ancient Silence her dominion keeps,
  Beyond the narrow boundaries of Time.
The taint of Sin, the vapors of the world,
  The smokes of godless altars, hang below,

Staining thy marge, but not a cloud is curled
  Where those supernal tides of ether flow.
What vistas ope from those serener plains!
  What dawning splendors touch thine azure towers!
  When some fair soul, whose path on Earth was ours
The starry freedom of its wing regains,
Shall it not linger for a moment there,
  One last divine regret to Earth returning,—
  One look, where Light ineffable is burning
      In Heaven's immortal Air!

VII.

Thine are the treasuries of Hail and Snow;
  Thy hand lets fall the Thunder's bolt of fire;
And when from out thy seething caldrons blow
  The vapors of the whirlwind, spire on spire
In terrible convolution wreathed and blent,
  The unimagined strength that lay concealed
  Within thy quiet bosom is revealed
To the racked Earth and trembling firmament.
And thou dost hold, awaiting God's decree,
  The keys of all destruction: — in that hour
  When the Almighty Wrath shall loose thy power,
Before thy breath shall disappear the sea,

To ashes turn the mountain's mighty frame,
  And as the seven-fold fervors wider roll,
  Thou, self-consuming, shrivel as a scroll,
And wrap the world in one wide pall of flame!

SONG.

Now the days are brief and drear:
Naked lies the new-born Year
In his cradle of the snow,
And the winds unbridled blow,
And the skies hang dark and low—
For the Summers come and go.

Leave the clashing cymbals mute!
Pipe no more the happy flute!
Sing no more that dancing rhyme
Of the rose's harvest-time—
Sing a requiem, sad and low:
For the Summers come and go.

Where is Youth? He strayed away
Through the meadow-flowers of May.

Where is Love? The leaves that fell
From his trysting-bower, can tell.
Wisdom stays, sedate and slow,
And the Summers come and go.

Yet a few more years to run,
Wheeling round in gloom and sun;
Other raptures, other woes —
Toil alternate with Repose:
Then to sleep where daisies grow,
While the Summers come and go.

THE MYSTERY.

Thou art not dead; thou art not gone to dust;
No line of all thy loveliness shall fall
To formless ruin, smote by Time, and thrust
Into the solemn gulf that covers all.

Thou canst not wholly perish, though the sod
Sink with its violets closer to thy breast;
Though by the feet of generations trod,
The head-stone crumbles from thy place of rest.

The marvel of thy beauty cannot die;
The sweetness of thy presence shall not fade;
Earth gave not all the glory of thine eye—
Death may not keep what Death has never made.

It was not thine, that forehead strange and cold,
  Nor those dumb lips, they hid beneath the snow;
Thy heart would throb beneath that passive fold,
  Thy hands for me that stony clasp forego.

But thou hadst gone — gone from the dreary land,
  Gone from the storms let loose on every hill,
Lured by the sweet persuasion of a hand
  Which leads thee somewhere in the distance still.

Where'er thou art, I know thou wearest yet
  The same bewildering beauty, sanctified
By calmer joy, and touched with soft regret
  For him who seeks, but cannot reach thy side.

I keep for thee the living love of old,
  And seek thy place in Nature, as a child
Whose hand is parted from his playmate's hold,
  Wanders and cries along a lonesome wild.

When, in the watches of my heart, I hear
  The messages of purer life, and know
The footsteps of thy spirit lingering near,
  The darkness hides the way that I should go.

Canst thou not bid the empty realms restore
  That form, the symbol of thy heavenly part?
Or on the fields of barren silence pour
  That voice, the perfect music of thy heart?

O once, once bending to these widowed lips,
  Take back the tender warmth of life from me,
Or let thy kisses cloud with swift eclipse
  The light of mine, and give me death with thee!

A PICTURE.

SOMETIMES, in sleeping dreams of night,
Or waking dreams of day,
The selfsame picture seeks my sight
And will not fade away.

I see a valley, cold and still,
Beneath a leaden sky:
The woods are leafless on the hill,
The fields deserted lie.

The gray November eve benumbs
The damp and cheerless air;
A wailing from the forest comes,
As of the world's despair.

But on the verge of night and storm,
  Far down the valley's line,
I see the lustre, red and warm,
  Of cottage windows shine.

And men are housed, and in their place,
  In snug and happy rest,
Save one, who walks with weary pace
  The highway's frozen breast.

His limbs, that tremble with the cold,
  Shrink from the coming storm;
But underneath his mantle's fold,
  His heart beats quick and warm.

He hears the laugh of those who sit
  In Home's contented air;
He sees the busy shadows flit
  Across the window's glare.

His heart is full of love unspent,
  His eyes are wet and dim;
For in those circles of content
  There is no room for him.

He clasps his hands and looks above;
  He makes the bitter cry:
"All, all are happy in their love—
  All are beloved but I!"

Across no threshold streams the light,
  Expectant, o'er his track;
No door is opened on the night,
  To bid him welcome back.

There is no other man abroad
  In all the wintry vale,
And lower upon his lonely road
  The darkness and the gale.

I see him through the doleful shades
  Press onward, sad and slow,
Till from my dream the picture fades,
  And from my heart the woe.

IN THE MEADOWS.

I LIE in the summer meadows,
 In the meadows all alone,
With the infinite sky above me
 And the sun on his mid-day throne.

The smell of the flowering grasses
 Is sweeter than any rose,
And a million happy insects
 Sing in the warm repose.

The mother lark that is brooding
 Feels the sun on her wings,
And the deeps of the noonday glitter
 With swarms of fairy things.

From the billowy green beneath me
To the fathomless blue above,
The creatures of God are happy
In the warmth of their summer love.

The infinite bliss of Nature
I feel in every vein;
The light and the life of Summer
Blossom in heart and brain.

But darker than any shadow
By thunder-clouds unfurled,
The awful truth arises,
That Death is in the world!

And the sky may beam as ever,
And never a cloud be curled;
And the airs be living odors,
But Death is in the world!

Out of the deeps of sunshine
The invisible bolt is hurled:
There's life in the summer meadows,
But Death is in the world!

SONNET.

THE soul goes forth and finds no resting place
On the wide breast of Life's unquiet sea
But in the heart of Man. The blazonry
Of Wealth and Power fades out, and leaves no trace;
Renown's fresh laurels for awhile may grace
The brow that wears them, but the dazzling tree
Has canker in its heart; Philosophy
Is not Content, and Art's immortal face
Is trenched with weary furrows: but the heart
Hoards in its cells the satisfying dew
Which all our thirst is powerless to exhaust.
Let Life's uncertain dignities depart,
And if one single manly heart be true,
My own, contented, counts them cheaply lost.

THE WINTER SOLSTICE.

O DARKEST day of all the year!
  O day of Winter and of Death!
Thy reign is in the North, yet here,
  The Southern Ocean feels thy breath.
Yon ruddy sun, that from the wave
  Climbs up his path in summer glow,
Will light, ere long, a frozen grave,
  Too cold to melt its pall of snow.

And I must find the sunshine pale,
  The tropic breezes chill and drear,
For when the gray autumnal gale
  Came to despoil the dying year,
Passed with the slow retreating sun,
  As day by day some beams depart,
The beauty and the life of one,
  Whose love made summer in my heart.

Day after day, the latest flower,
  Her faded being waned away,
More pale and dim with every hour—
  And ceased upon the darkest day!
The warmth and glow that with her died
  No light of coming suns shall bring;
The heart its wintry gloom may hide,
  But cannot feel a second Spring.

O darkest day of all the year!
  In vain thou com'st with balmy skies,
For, blotting out their azure sphere,
  The phantoms of my Fate arise:
A blighted life, whose shattered plan
  No after fortune can restore;
The perfect lot, designed for Man,
  That should be mine, but is no more.

She was the sun, that rose above
  The landscape of the life I dreamed,
And through the portals of her love
  The promise of my Future beamed.
Though buried long, those dreams arise
  To mock me wheresoe'er I roam—
The happy light of household eyes,
  The blessing and the peace of Home.

And I behold the changing fire
  Of alien heavens increase and pale
On many a sunbeam-gilded spire
  And many a moonlight-silvered sail :
The pomp and glory of the lands,
  The range of Earth, is given to me ;
But every touch of loving hands
  Recalls my blighted destiny.

IN ARTICULO MORTIS.

I WOULD be left alone — with none but you,
The last, sole friend, where all have fallen off
Like summer birds, and left your nest alone
Amidst the withered foliage of my heart.
Give me your hand : your soul will walk with mine
Into the shadows, far as life may go
Within the porch of Death, and send its cry
Of faithful love across the mighty gulf,
When we are forced asunder.

Nay, Priest ! nay :
Stand not between me and the fading light
Of my last hour. I know my soul is weighed
With many sins — the pages of my life
Soiled with unworthy records ; that I go
Redder than scarlet to the awful bar
Where God shall judge me : but even, knowing this,
And stung with wild, unutterable woe,

As the lost chances of my life arise,
With all their opportunities of good
Deepening the blackness of the evil choice,
I will not lean upon another's arm,
Or lift my soul upon another's prayer,
Or bid a human intercessor plead
My perilous cause ; but I will stagger on,
Beneath my sins, unto the feet of God,
For, were the crushing burden tenfold great,
He sees the secret heart which they obscure
And not withholds His mercy. He is just,
And I am sick of human justice. I
Will go to Him, who sent me on the earth
Wisely, though I have trampled on His gifts ;
In love, though I have tasted most of pain ;
And justly, though the monstrous wrongs that men
Perpetuate in His name have borne me down
Beyond all virtue, but my faith in Him.
Go, Priest ! the absolution which I seek
No prayer of yours can purchase : I have gone
Beyond your reach already, and the last
Weak props of life one after one give way.

O father — father ! In what fatal school
Learned you the iron creed that drove your child,
Sore with the scourging of its rigid laws,

To the alluring license of the world ?
Why did you crush the healthy joys that craved
Growth in a liberal air, the motions free
That leap along the bounding pulse of Youth
And pluck delight in the fresh fields of Time,
Building your stern religion round the dreams
That fill, self-born, the morning sleep of Life,
And give us courage for its day of toil ?
Had you not hedged each simple joy with sin,
And from the guileless blooms of Nature driven
My steps, to falter on your arid wastes
Of harshest duty, I had never looked
To Sin for joy, nor plunged amid the rank,
Dense overgrowths of Pleasure, which conceal
Her soundless quicksands : had you turned the tide
Of warm, impetuous blood, that beat so strong
In every vein, to mingle with the streams
Of manly action, I had spent its force
In watering many a pleasant field of life
With fertilizing increase ; but you set
Your unrelenting dogmas in its path,
Locked the dark barrier with a cruel hand,
And thought the fierce rebellion you provoked
By tyranny against my nature's law,
The evidence of Hell ! The buttressed walls
You built to stay me madly burst away,

And like a captive by recovered light
Blinded, and in the long-lost airs of Heaven
Reeling inebriate, I was tossed along
Upon a flood I knew not how to stem,
Through the wide sea of desolating years,
Until the flying wreck on which you hurled
Your stern anathemas, is thrown at last,
A heap of ruin, on the barren shores
Where the world's outcasts take their bitter leave
Of the cold world's injustice.

Wholly lost
Not then was I, O father! had you shown
The awful pathos of a father's grief,
Or dropped one word that spoke a father's love,
Bursting, as from a heart at lava-glow,
Through the cold wrath that made you adamant,
In that brief time, when loathingly I turned
From the palled company of Vice, to throw
My heart, repentant, at the feet of one
Who might have lifted me from out the deeps,
And set my feet upon the steady paths
I labored to recover. But, when you,
My father, spurned and drove me back to sin,
You snapped the feeble chain to which I clung,
And she, and you, and all the blinded world —

O God, how blind! — you saw me fall, and fall,
And loosed my frantic clutch from every prop
Until the floods above my head were rolled
So deep, I bade farewell to light and took
My portion with the darkness. You have passed
To other life already: I will think
You did but deal with me as you were taught
By heartless laws of Sect, which you mistook
For Heaven's commandments. In this solemn hour
Death washes out the bitterness that filled
The Past, and I forgive: — God! that a son
Should ever have such need!

She, whom I found
Amid those dreary haunts where brazen Sin
Laughed o'er her fall from virtue — she, whose love,
Her only weakness, to the brink betrayed
Where one blind step condemns to endless woe —
She was not false: she threw before my feet
Her bruised and trampled heart, and from the wrecks
Of outraged tenderness built up anew
The shrine of Love, the saddened counterfeit
Of that, which from the bowers of innocent hearts
Sends the pure incense of its perfect joy
To God's high throne. She clung to me with truth
That might have cleansed her from the stains of shame,

Were Man less cruel. Hunted, driven to bay
By persecution and by keenest want,
She spurned the tempters who would blight the last
Pale flower, that in her ravaged fields of life
Recalled the happy days when she was pure.
Rest thee, thou weary spirit! Were there tears
In the cold eyes of men, thy touching faith
Should draw them forth, and gentlest Charity,
Veiling thy frailties, leave thy memory white
With the redemption of that saving love!
You, too, my friend — (still keep my hand in yours,
For we are nigh the parting) — you were true,
Faithful where all were faithless. In the dark
Which filled the chambers of my soul, you saw
The wreck of manliness that might have been,
Capacities for love which never came,
And the deserted shrines whence Faith had fled:
But you alike had suffered from the laws
That wrought such devastation; you had felt
In suffering, the kind regard of Heaven,
And all the guilty records of my life
Knit you the closer, till your love became
The agent of God's pity. I will think
He shall not wholly cast me off, nor doom
My soul to endless company with sins
I loathed while I committed: that, if He

Shut His bright Heaven against me, there may be
Among his myriad worlds some lonely place,
Though far remote, within the radiant sphere
His glory blesses, where she waits for me,
And you will join us in a little while.
He gave us to each other : will He now
Break the sweet links whereby we felt our hearts
First drawn to Him ? He, the All-Merciful,
Who not deserted us when men forsook,
And loved when they despised us, will not judge
Too harshly, when our naked souls go up
To meet His awful presence.

* * * *

I am chill,
And the room darkens : let me feel your hand
Here, where my heart beats feebly. Friend — dear friend !
Kiss me upon the cheek, before it grows
Too cold, and lift my head upon your breast.
Tears on my face ? The scalding tears of man,
Not lightly shattered from their iron cells,
Shed thus for me ? It sweetens Death, to know
Such rain as this will consecrate my dust.

SATURDAY NIGHT AT SEA.

COME, messmates, fill the cheerful bowl!
  To-night let no one fail,
No matter how the billows roll,
  Or roars the ocean gale.
There's toil and danger in our lives,
  But let us jovial be,
And drink to sweethearts and to wives,
  On Saturday night at sea!

The chill nor'wester hurls the spray
  Our icy bulwarks o'er,
As swift we cleave our stormy way,
  A thousand miles from shore;
And while the good ship onward drives,
  Let none forget that he
Must drink to sweethearts and to wives,
  On Saturday night at sea!

The joys that landsmen little reck
  We best can understand,
Who live a year upon the deck,
  A month upon the land.
And rough as are our sailor lives,
  Full tender hearts have we
To drink to sweethearts and to wives,
  On Saturday night at sea!

Our frames are worn and little worth,
  And hard our rugged hands;
We struggle for our hold on Earth
  With the storms of many lands:
But the only love that lights our lives
  Shall still remembered be;
We drink to sweethearts and to wives,
  On Saturday night at sea!

SONG.

They call thee false as thou art fair,
They call thee fair and free —
A creature pliant as the air
And changeful as the sea :
But I, who gaze with other eyes —
Who stand and watch afar,
Behold thee pure as yonder skies
And steadfast as a star !

Thine is a rarer nature, born
To rule the common crowd,
And thou dost lightly laugh to scorn
The hearts before thee bowed.
Thou dreamest of a different love
Than comes to such as these ;
That soars as high as heaven above
Their shallow sympathies.

A star that shines with flickering spark,
  Thou dost not wane away,
But shed'st adown the purple dark
  The fulness of thy ray:
A rose, whose odors freely part
  At every zephyr's will,
Thou keep'st within thy folded heart
  Its virgin sweetness still!

THE MID-WATCH.

I PACE the deck in the dead of night,
  When the moon and starlight fail,
And the cordage creaks to the lazy swells,
  And heavily flaps the sail.
On the darkness glimmers the binnacle-lamp
  With feeble and lonely spell :
No sound but the passing sentry's tramp
  Or his measured cry : "All's well!"

To and fro, with accustomed step,
  I walk in the night alone,
And I think of a thousand watches kept
  In the years forever flown ;
Of the friends in whose manly fellowship
  I labored long ago,
Till Death relieved their watch on earth,
  And they went to rest below.

I think of the gallant ones who died
  When our broadsides shook the sea,
And sorrow for them subdued the pride
  Of our cheers of victory:
Of those who fell in the fevered lands,
  Or sank in the whelming wave —
Whose corpses waste on the barren sands,
  Or float in a fathomless grave.

And the looks revive that were faint and dim
  In the shadows of the years,
And I scan them o'er till my eyelids swim
  With the strange delight of tears:
They people the dark with their pallid brows
  As they silently throng around,
And the sea its phosphor radiance throws
  On the faces of the drowned.

So many a noble heart is cold
  That shared my duties then,
I have looked full oft in the face of Death,
  But he comes to better men;
And let him come in his chosen time,
  Some friend will think of me,
And I shall live in the lonely hours
  Of his midnight watch at sea.

THE PHANTOM.

Again I sit within the mansion,
In the old, familiar seat;
And shade and sunshine chase each other
O'er the carpet at my feet.

But the sweet-brier's arms have wrestled upwards
In the summers that are past,
And the willow trails its branches lower
Than when I saw them last.

They strive to shut the sunshine wholly
From out the haunted room;
To fill the house, that once was joyful,
With silence and with gloom.

And many kind, remembered faces
  Within the doorway come —
Voices, that wake the sweeter music
  Of one that now is dumb.

They sing, in tones as glad as ever,
  The songs she loved to hear ;
They braid the rose in summer garlands,
  Whose flowers to her were dear.

And still, her footsteps in the passage,
  Her blushes at the door,
Her timid words of maiden welcome,
  Come back to me once more.

And, all forgetful of my sorrow,
  Unmindful of my pain,
I think she has but newly left me,
  And soon will come again.

She stays without, perchance, a moment,
  To dress her dark-brown hair ;
I hear the rustle of her garments —
  Her light step on the stair !

O, fluttering heart! control thy tumult,
  Lest eyes profane should see
My cheeks betray the rush of rapture
  Her coming brings to me!

She tarries long: but lo! a whisper
  Beyond the open door,
And, gliding through the quiet sunshine,
  A shadow on the floor!

Ah! 'tis the whispering pine that calls me,
  The vine, whose shadow strays;
And my patient heart must still await her,
  Nor chide her long delays.

But my heart grows sick with weary waiting,
  As many a time before:
Her foot is ever at the threshold,
  Yet never passes o'er.

LAMENT AND CONSOLATION.

FALSE, fleeting Youth, ah! whither fled
Thy golden promise?
Thy joy is past, thy love is dead,
And every arrowy hope we sped
Falls distant from us.

Ah, where the wondrous alchemy
Thy steps that haunted?
The happy airs of Arcady
That fanned thy brow, the fancy free,
The faith undaunted?

The glories caught from Nature die,
And men deceive me;
Star after star goes down the sky,
And darker, sadder hours are nigh,
If Song should leave me.

For Song can still the living light
Of Memory borrow,
With faded dawns to flush the night,
And hide with gleams of old delight
The present sorrow.

Let Faith and Love and Hope depart,
Since Fate so wills it :
Some foliage yet may shade the heart,
And blossom in the beams of Art,
Whose presence fills it.

On thee, dear Song! the loss I cast,
Beyond redressing :
Let gone be gone, and past be past,
But, Angel! I will hold thee fast,
And force thy blessing!

www.ingramcontent.com/pod-product-compliance
Lightning Source LLC
LaVergne TN
LVHW011217110826
845150LV00006B/1451

* 9 7 8 1 4 2 5 5 1 6 6 9 7 *